JUMPSEAT

JET-SETTING IN THE 70S

Sharing my memories with your imagination

DIANNA BENNETT

CONTENTS

INTRODUCTION

AN OVERVIEW OF TRAVEL IN THE 70'S

"Between 1955 and 1972, passenger numbers more than quadrupled. By 1972 almost half of Americans had flown although most passengers were business travelers."

– The National Air and Space Museum

In the 1950's, the average American family traveled by car to their vacation spots like Disneyland and the Grand Canyon. They spent hours on dusty roads in hot, cramped station wagons, reading billboards and playing car games as they bumped along Route 66. Drive-in restaurants like Burger King and McDonald's popped up as families discovered fast food in their slow cars.

When it came to flying, the businessmen, or their companies, could afford to pay the exorbitant first-class fees. They dressed in their suits and enjoyed champagne from crystal glasses while comfortably sitting in spacious seats, enduring the stares of the peasants passing by on their way to the coach cabin.

Each airline enthusiastically courted their potential travelers with the best food, the prettiest girls, and the wildest advertisements. It was the era of *Mad Men* advertising, and there were no limits to enticing a new customer. The repeat customers joined airline clubs, which eventually turned them into "frequent flyers." A frequent flyer was treated like royalty, and there were so few back then. These individuals had attained an exclusive status that would reap benefits for their companies – their repeat travel could lead to lower fares.

The price of an airline ticket was fixed and regulated by the Civil Aeronautics Board (CAB). This was an agency of the federal government, located in Washington D.C., that was formed in 1938 and abolished in 1985. The CAB regulated aviation services (including scheduled passenger services.) It was replaced by the Federal Aviation Administration (FAA) in August 23, 1958.

TWA also put an emphasis on hiring the best chefs and the most beautiful women. For the hostesses, they placed height, weight and age limits on each of the applicants. They warned that marriage was a "no-no," and that mandatory termination would happen at age 32.

The earliest airlines used first officers to serve cold sandwiches and hot coffee to passengers in bumpy, noisy Ford Trimotors and DC 3s. As flights became more complicated, it occurred to management that perhaps the pilot should remain in the cockpit. The first officers were then replaced by young, handsome men called stewards.

According to the National Aviation Museum, a nurse from Iowa, Ellen Church, wanted to become an airline pilot, but realized that was not possible for a woman in her day. So, in 1930, she approached Steve Simpson at Boeing Air Transport with the novel idea of placing nurses aboard airlines. She convinced him that the presence of women nurses would help relieve the traveling public's fear of flying. Since Boeing was owned by United Airlines, she was the first woman to join the newly designated title of stewardess. The addition of female nurses in the cabin fundamentally changed the flying experience.

Few people could afford to travel back then. When you consider the price of an airline ticket represented nearly 20% of the average salary, it was understandable. They never dreamed that one day; a man would make air travel affordable for the common man.

Juan Trippe, the president of Pan American Airlines, was that man. His legacy included introducing the "tourist class" into the jargon of airline pricing. This, along with the introduction of jet travel, eventually caused the price of a ticket to become attainable to a blue-collar worker, although still not quite affordable. Trippe's relentless pursuit of larger and faster jets would change the dynamics of travel and would eventually make the common man's dreams of travel come true.

Pan Am, with the famous Clipper Flying boats, was the first airline to cross the Pacific. Trippe's tenacious desire to open new routes for airmail became instrumental in exploring Hong Kong, Hawaii, and Pago Pago for the wealthy to visit. Years later, these destinations would grow into vacation hot spots.

Trippe spearheaded the Boeing 707 with its inaugural flight to Paris from New York in 1958. He relentlessly cajoled and prodded the president of Boeing, William Allen, to build the 747; "If I build it, will you buy it" was repeated by Allen to Trippe on many occasions. This dream, this enormous airplane, would propel the public across the oceans, and it would change the fabric of the airlines. It would also make Trippe a legend.

On January 21, 1970, the first regularly scheduled commercial flight of the 747 took place. Clipper Young America was scheduled to make the inaugural flight from JFK to London, but an engine failure resulted in a several-hour delay, and a replacement aircraft was summoned. This did not spoil the enthusiasm of the flying public, however, as they watched the jet rumble down the runway.

The "Jumbo Jet," as it was lovingly called, changed the landscape and fabric of airports. In the beginning, there were few airports that could manage the problems that the 747 created. The jumbos were parked on the ramps, and newly designed air stairs were used until jetways could be implemented. Passengers were sometimes unhappy having to walk outside – until they turned around to marvel at the size of the plane.

When a 747 failed to perform, there was immediate chaos. Instead of a mere 100 passengers needing attention, there were as many as 400. More agents had to be hired, and more mechanics trained, not to mention pilots.

Short layovers for crews expanded into days, since additional time was needed for the cleaning crews and mechanics to accomplish their routine tasks.

The cabin crew complement was a minimum of 14 to 16 hostesses on each flight, nearly three times the number of cabin crew needed on the Boeing 707. A call went out to hire more women and *fast*.

TWA, Pan Am's main competitor, flew its first 747 on February 25, 1970, from Los Angeles to New York. It was not quite as auspicious as Pan Am's first flight. The call from TWA went out to hire more people.

I answered that call on January 17, 1970.

CHAPTER ONE

DUMPED

"Sometimes good things fall apart so better things can fall together."

– Marilyn Monroe

Southern California Bible College, a small parochial school nestled among the residents of Costa Mesa, California, was built piece by piece as donations appeared from churches around the state. Its antiquated buildings and occasional trailers were partially hidden among the palm trees that lined the campus. A lonely flag announced its affiliation with the Assemblies of God, a Pentecostal group that promoted strict Ten Commandment adherence. It served as a beacon of salvation to those of us lost to the sinful sirens of the Beatles and the gyrations of the Rolling Stones.

I needed a beacon. The lustful tug of the beach had confused my saintly mind. My guardians, sensing this, rushed me headlong into the doors of this quiet college. They hoped that the aseptic campus would help me follow my religious calling.

God had blessed me with good looks and a decent singing voice. Oral Roberts University had wooed me with free admittance in exchange for unfettered access to my talent, but Oklahoma wasn't attractive enough to entice me away. To make matters worse, I had met a young man and fallen in love. Vince didn't go to church or profess any faith, so I knew I had to keep our relationship on the down low.

We met on a ski holiday. It was spring break, and several friends and I were all itching for an adventure. The news of freshly fallen snow at Big Bear Mountain enticed a few of us to pool our money for gas and snacks, and fortunately a parent had "gifted" us a five-bedroom cabin for two days.

As we began our trek up the mountain, we spotted Vince and his brother sitting on the side of the road next to their broken-down truck. It was an easy decision to leave the truck and take the men with us.

Later, we all laughed as we fell down the bunny slopes, under the influence of apple wine.

Vince possessed everything that the Hollywood magazines had primed me to look for: he was tall, dark, and handsome, with a smile that sizzled my body and eyes that seared my born-again soul. I loved his infectious enthusiasm for life, and his toxic humor about death. He was sinful and he was wild – he was everything I was taught to run away from.

The only problem was that he and his brother were celebrating their two weeks before they entered Camp Pendleton. It was the calling, the faraway war that he had signed up for; Vietnam changed the direction of so many young men in 1969.

Before basic training, he invited me to drive up the Pacific Coast Highway to see his parents in Oregon. The sky was so blue and the sun so penetrating that we had to close the roof on his red Corvette. We stopped to buy Dungeness crab from a roadside vendor and sipped Cold Duck while crashing waves filled the deep-carved caves that lined the beach far below. A fine, salty spray filled my lungs as I muffled my cries of fear mixed with screams of joy as he pushed the Corvette to its limits.

It was glorious, and I knew we were meant to be.

When he left for Vietnam, I was devastated. I never believed he'd return – so many young men didn't, after all.

For 13 months I stalked the mailman, hoping for a letter from him. His letters were both passionate and sad. He was evolving into an anti-war soldier, and his comments eventually gained recognition from the censors' black marks. I, on the other hand, was becoming aware that my focus was on the six o'clock news and the war.

When he did return from his tour, he had changed. The happy, smiling man was now sullen, jumpy, and no longer interested in marriage. He didn't tell me, but he proved this by failing to appear at the wedding he had agreed to.

Months after returning the wedding dress and gifts, I received a late-night phone call from Vince. The conversation was short: if I wanted an explanation from him, I would need to fly to Seattle, where he was now based. He had decided to stay in the Marine Corps.

I had never flown on an airplane, and I knew nothing about them, but I knew I had to get an answer from him. His mysterious disappearance kept me awake at night.

For some unexplainable reason, I drove to the local grocery store to find boxes, and then proceeded to pack up all my clothing. I arrived at the airport with six boxes festooned with colorful labels for bananas and an overused, over-packed suitcase.

They say love makes you blind – it makes you stupid, too.

I was sold a standby ticket. Not having much money, it seemed like a steal. The United Airlines agent tried to warn me about the word "standby," but I wasn't listening.

I hadn't given a thought to flying until I sat down in the small seat of the jet. My thoughts were on my family and what they would think of this – would they think that I was brave or stupid?

It must have been obvious that I had never flown; my seatmate explained all the sounds that made me jump instinctively. After two hours we landed safely, and I asked for his help in getting a cab.

I felt so very grown up handing the taxicab driver the address for my rendezvous. My love – oh how sweet that sounds – had paid for the motel room in advance. It all seemed so perfect.

Until I arrived. The hotel was long past its glory. The cab's tires crunched on the pebbles that lined the entrance of the dilapidated hotel. Unpainted shutters hung precariously near windows that must have once enjoyed the few sunny days of Washington state. The sidewalk crumbled in long shallow pools of dirt and human waste.

Brochures sitting on the dust-covered nightstand portrayed a much different rendition of the fleabag hotel that I was sitting in; there were photos of families frolicking in a crystal-clear pool. I looked at the pool from my window, and even with the burned-out lights it had seen better days. Long-forgotten lounge chairs floated aimlessly with the accumulated leaves. The smiling hotel agent on the brochure wasn't remotely like the unhappy, unkept man who begrudgingly left *The Price is Right* on T.V. while he checked me in.

How could Vince have booked this place for our meeting? I was confused – was this a sign that I refused to see?

The room was so filthy, I decided to stay in my clothing. After removing the stained bedspread, I sat atop the sheets. A cockroach played havoc with my anxiety as I watched it invite his relatives to join the party near my baggage.

My watch told me the story. As I strained with every sound to hear his approach, I knew at midnight that he wasn't coming. I began to cry, then sob. After hours of tears, I was resolute. Even if I had his phone number, which I didn't, I was done. Going back home, even with all its challenges, sounded good. I woke up my temperamental hotel agent and he begrudgingly called a cab.

With no one to help, I carried my possessions to the curb, where I heaped them in an untidy pile that perfectly represented my mood. I sat on the edge of the curb, precariously close to a mess of garbage distributed the night before. I *looked* a mess, like I belonged there. My clothes were wrinkled from hours of wear. My makeup was streaking down my face, and uncontrollable tears continued to fall.

When the cab arrived, and the driver's face became visible, I smiled. He, a diminutive Japanese man, left his car and greeted me as I stood and stretched. "Good morning, Miss."

I was so happy to see a familiar face – he had driven me to this hell hole the night before.

"So, it's back to the airport for you?" he asked.

"Yes, it's back to the airport. And back to L.A."

"What time is your flight?"

"Eight o'clock."

"Same airline? United, wasn't it?"

He did not ask why I was leaving so soon. The drive was long enough, and experience told him that I would talk; his curiosity would be fed in due time.

The luggage arrangement was identical to the night before. Once again, he methodically repacked four of the large boxes into the trunk of his cab. Two more were placed in the front seat, leaving me in the back next to my suitcase.

He returned to the driver's seat and watched me from the rearview mirror. "Ready?" he asked.

"I have been ready since midnight."

The cab slowly made its way onto the paved road. Looking back at the hotel, I was surprised at how even more dreadful it looked in the daylight.

How could my former fiancé have suggested a dump like this? Perhaps that was just another clue in this ill-fated rendezvous. "A neutral place" was the phrase he had used the day before, a term used during a war, or perhaps an armistice. Our last conversation was so scattered and tangled with signals that it took an evening alone in a room to untie the threads of this betrayal. I now knew that my longing to see him after 13 months had clouded my judgment. The warning bells were drowned by the wedding bells that played in my head.

The driver spoke: "Seattle-Tacoma International Airport, or Sea-Tac as it is commonly called, was developed as a direct response to the Japanese attack on Pearl Harbor on December 7, 1941."

"Really? That's interesting…I mean, it's interesting that you would know that and you're Japanese."

He laughed. "Yes, many tourists say that. Regardless of who you are, history is still history. You can't change the past, only the future." He smiled.

I smiled back. "May I ask your name? I mean, I forgot to ask last night. And you were so kind to listen to me."

"My name is Kazuo."

"Kazuo," I repeated.

"It means 'man of peace.' My mother wanted me to be a priest. I never wanted to be a priest, though. I became a cab driver after the war. In many ways I became what my mother wanted, I just don't wear the robes or hang out in temples." He laughed.

"How lovely. I mean, your name."

After a long silence he decided to ask the obvious: "So your young man didn't show last night?"

"No." Tears welled again in the rims of my reddened eyes. "Not even a phone call. It's so unlike him to do this. I hope nothing bad happened to him."

"I doubt it. He just returned from Vietnam; didn't you say? Men are sometimes very stupid. I am sure he will have a very good reason for this. At least I hope so." He looked back this time and handed me a tissue. "So, what are you going to do now?"

"Go back home, to L.A. I can't return to school. I told everyone I was going off to get married, and I'll never live it down. Damn, I wish he'd died in Vietnam. At least I'd have my dignity."

I blew my nose. I was immediately sorry for saying that. "I'm sorry I didn't mean that. I'm just very confused and tired."

"It's okay; I understand. You know, no one must know what happened here. Keep your dignity, go on with your life. Many of us have had to do that, you know? My family was very wealthy when World War Two broke out. My father died of shame when the Japanese bombed Pearl Harbor, and my mother died right after him. Then my sister and I were locked up in a prison camp because of our nationality. You must make the best of your life, it's all you have."

As the taxi made its way through the twists and turns of the airport terminals, I watched this graying man's eyes as he glanced back at me. I decided maybe he was right.

As the morning sun won the battle over the fog, my sadness slowly began to change to anger.

Long lines of uniformed soldiers queued outside the terminal, waiting their turn to check in at the skycap counter on the curb. Sadness squeezed my heart.

The cab stopped in front. I tugged on my large suitcase as it clung greedily to the taxi.

One of the young soldiers noticed me. "Need some help?"

I smiled back, "No thanks, not today."

After the bags were delivered to the sky cap, I turned to speak to Kazuo.

"Thank you for listening to me. You were very kind. I will take advantage of your wisdom, if you don't mind?" I reached to shake his hand.

"Remember, life is very short – make the most of it. Do you have enough money to get home?"

"Oh, I'll be fine, thank you." I watched as he drove away. What a nice man he was to care about me.

The baggage agent frenetically tagged my bags. "I'm sorry miss. There's a troop movement today. They're all going to Vietnam." I tipped him my last dollar.

When I appeared at the gate, I was advised that I would have to wait for a seat. I now knew what the word "standby" meant: the flights were full, and I would be waiting all day for a flight back home. Exhausted from lack of sleep, and hungry, I made my way to the bathroom to freshen up.

A very attractive woman, dressed in an extremely short orange jumper with white go-go boots, appeared at the sink. Her red hair and red lipstick accentuated her unusual appearance.

"Where are you based?" she asked, as she washed her perfectly manicured hands.

"Based?" I said. "I don't understand."

"Oh, I'm sorry. I just assumed you were a stewardess. Like me."

"No. I'm just a person who is incapable of understanding men."

She laughed. "Well girl, join the club. Have you eaten breakfast? You look a little peaked." I couldn't help noticing her southern drawl.

I explained that I was out of money, having spent it all on cabs and tips, plus I was on "standby", and I was afraid I wasn't going to get home.

She smiled. "My treat." After some cajoling, I agreed.

The airport was chaos with all the military wandering about. All the restaurants had long lines. Eventually, we descended downstairs into a large room under the airport which she called a "Crew Cafeteria." I'd later learn that this is where flight attendants came to eat, complain about the passengers, or just get away from the crowds. The room was filled with different uniforms representing many different airlines.

I soon found myself seated at breakfast, being cheered up by this kind airline stewardess. Her name was Anne Marie, and she flew for

Continental Airlines. She explained that she was in Seattle to visit her parents and was now on her way back to Houston, where she worked and lived.

She convinced me to tell her why I was crying. My story wasn't new to her; she explained that this type of betrayal was happening all over. Vietnam changes young men. She asked what my plans were.

My life was a wreck; I had no plans.

"You need to get a job as a stewardess and show this loser what a fool he was for dumping you, not once but twice. Pay him back with a life of excitement and fun. Believe me, you are definitely the type they are looking for. TWA is hiring right now, and they are just beginning to fly the 747. When you get home, investigate this. It will change your life."

"But what will I tell my family and my friends?"

"Why do they need to know? It's your life. Promise me that you will call TWA when you get home. Hey, and that "standby" thing – stop worrying. That's the way I travel. Sometimes it's risky, but it's free for crew members. Now give me a big Texas hug."

We embraced. When I pulled away, she smiled. "I'll see you in the sky," she said.

A wise man and a stewardess had just changed the direction of my life. I would forget Vince. I would call TWA. That was my new plan.

CHAPTER TWO

LOST LUGGAGE

I phoned my friend for a ride home from the airport. As I expected, she immediately started with the questions. I promised that I'd explain later and was grateful when the dime fell into the phone collection box, ending our call.

So, there I stood: waiting for my bags after eight hours of traveling. The now-empty baggage carousel mocked me as it continued moving. The recorded message, "the white zone is for loading and unloading only; no parking" reverberated in my head. What had been a congested arena of people fighting for their bags now resembled a ghost town.

I was the only person left without a suitcase or box to my name. As an orange cone appeared, signaling the end of the bags, I was devastated. I had been asking for some help from God, and I was now questioning my faith.

A uniformed man collected the cone. "I'm sorry, miss, there aren't any more bags coming up."

I tried to reply, but nothing came out of my mouth.

"You need to go and talk to our baggage agent." He pointed to a sign that read "United Airlines Lost Baggage."

Lost baggage! *Oh, please don't let my bags be lost*, I repeated in my head, over and over, as I made my way to the room. That would be just too much to take after the past 24 hours of emotional hell.

An older, uniformed man wearing spectacles stared at me from the lost baggage office. The small room's walls were covered with photographs of suitcases.

"Do you have your baggage tags?" he asked.

I handed him my collection of tickets and tags. After what seemed like an eternity of typing, he spoke, but with venom coating his words, and bereft of empathy. "Did you really have this many bags?" he asked incredulously.

"Yes. I had six boxes and one suitcase." In some small way, I was happy to know that he might know how many of my valuables were missing.

"Well, did anyone charge you extra for all of this luggage?"

Before I could respond, he mumbled, "No, probably not; pretty girls always get away with breaking the rules. But someone should have charged you extra for all of this."

"I'm sorry, I didn't know. This is my first experience with flying," I said.

He smirked, "Well, ignorance is no excuse. I really should charge you now."

Rage sat, percolating, ready to pounce on him at any moment. "Do you have my bags?" I asked quietly.

"No, actually I haven't had the pleasure of picking up six boxes and a suitcase for anyone today." Now his smirk was a smile, a truly evil smile.

At this point, I wanted to reach over the counter and choke this little prick, but I reconsidered, since at this moment, he was in control of my clothing.

"What took you so long to come and get your bags?" he asked. "You should have been here hours ago."

I stood looking at him. *He couldn't be this stupid*, I thought. I knew little about the airlines, but I believed he must know that I had been stuck in Seattle for hours.

"Your airline bumped me this morning. I have been waiting at the airport since 8:00 a.m."

"We didn't bump you. The military bumped you."

"Listen, I just want my bags and I want to go home. Where are my bags?" I pleaded.

"I wish I knew. We haven't got one of your bags here. I'll take some information, and when and *if* we find them, we'll let you know."

"Everything I own is in those boxes." I could feel the tears welling up in my tired eyes.

He stared at me, emotionless. If I was waiting for some sympathy or empathy from him, I would have a very long wait coming.

"I need to warn you that we've had luggage stolen from the airport lately, especially when we have full flights. People come in from off the street and load up their cars. The airport assigned us security guards, but it's hard to tell a passenger from a thief. They're supposed to check bag tags, but I doubt they are."

As I walked away, I felt numb.

When I saw my car at the curb, with my friend behind the wheel, I felt at home again. So much had happened in the last 24 hours that I had forgotten how much I missed L.A. I even missed this 'Chatty Kathy', who was probably already preparing to call everyone and share the gossip after she dropped me off.

As she reached to hug me, she muttered. "I'm glad you're here. These airport cops are none too friendly,"

I got in the car, and she wasted no time. "So, what are you doing back so soon?" she asked.

"They lost my bags."

She shook her head. "That doesn't make sense. I asked why you are back so soon."

"I'll tell you later. I desperately need some sleep."

"They lost your bags. That's why you're back?" She maneuvered the car down to the freeway ramp.

"Not just my bags – my clothes, my books, my shoes, my underwear, all of my everything." The reality of the betrayal and the loss of my worldly belongings began to sink in.

"So why are you back so soon?" What happened? I mean, I was shocked when my mom said you called."

"Listen, I'll explain it all after I get some sleep. Can I stay at your place tonight? I don't want to face my family yet."

"Sure!" I could hear the elation in her voice.

CHAPTER THREE

REDONDO BEACH

Have you ever felt the earth shift beneath your feet? I experienced a jolt or two while living in California. We all lived knowing someday the "Big One" – the San Andreas Fault – would be our undoing. But as I lay in my friend's bed later that night, unable to sleep, I realized that a different kind of shift had just occurred in my life: I no longer had a plan, a future husband, or even clothing.

As the sun began to rise, it was time to address the last 24 hours. My friend would most likely return at any moment from her boyfriend's house, and she would want answers, but I wasn't ready to talk to anyone.

There was only one place where I could sit, think and plan. It was the ocean, the quiet, non-judgmental constant in my young life. When I moved to California from Texas – an abandoned child, a survivor from a violent, alcoholic family – I had found my sanity here. This was where I felt safe and free of obligations.

I arrived. Leaving the comfort of my car, I fed a nickel in the meter. I found a familiar bench near the sand. The wood was cool and comforting, and I longed for the morning sun's restorative rays. Doing its best to divide the morning fog, it moved over the rows of the multi-colored beach houses that crowded onto the sandy, sloping hills.

It seems little had changed here since I left for college. The same orphaned bikes lay on their sides among the patches of nutrient-starved grass. Overflowing trash cans spilled onto the sand as seagulls happily engorged themselves on the remnants of the previous night's revelry. Mounds of seaweed, mingled with bits of garbage that had managed to escape the evening tides, awaited the tractors poised to clean the beach.

A small group of local surfers began to arrive slowly, surveying the ocean and searching it for the waves they coveted in preparation for their daily sport. Their "Woodys" were parked lovingly and illegally along the narrow, winding streets. Any other time this would solicit fear of a ticket from the cops, but parking tickets had become trivial in this new world order. The ascending number on the young men's draft cards replaced any fear of a $5 parking ticket.

I watched as they donned their protective wet suits and ran headlong into the sea. Laying on their boards, their feet and hands paddling the cool water, and the morning sun glistening off their black wet suits, they resembled seals. Sharks had been known to make this same comparison.

Occasionally, a cry, possibly of a shark attack, interrupted the calm. It rippled through the group of young men. Heads turned in the direction of the sound, but soon they were back to their quest. One by one, over and over, they tried to ride the sometimes-unproductive waves, often falling headlong into the sea. I admired their determination.

At this hour, the beachside shops were readying themselves for tourists. The sand had to be swept from the front doors and signs erected in anticipation of their arrival.

The sounds of a song by the group Iron Butterfly echoed through the seaside bungalows, and the aroma of marijuana wafted in the sea breeze. The song, In- a-Gadda-Da-Vida, had been a rallying cry for an anti-war group that gathered on the beach every night; protests against the Vietnam War were common here.

A jet appeared overhead, flashing in the sun, and I was reminded of last night's betrayal. I needed to go home and face my reality.

Back in the car, I turned on the radio, and I was once again assailed by the TWA advertisement. It seemed to play constantly on every station. The announcer invited me to try my hand at flying on airplanes, anywhere and everywhere.

This time, remembering my promise to the stewardess, Anne Marie, I wrote the number down. It was time to try my hand at a new profession.

Leaving the beach, I knew it was time to follow through on my promise. My biggest fear was another rejection. God knows, I'd had my share lately. Maybe I was too tall, or they'd somehow realize over the phone how naïve I was. I returned to my home, knowing my family were all at work, and dialed the number.

Before I could chicken out, a voice answered: "Good morning, TWA, can I help you?"

"Yes, I'd like to apply for the air hostess position, please."

The voice over the phone was professional as she asked questions designed for this unique job:

"Are you over 18 years of age? Do you have 20/20 vision? Are you over five-foot-two and under five-foot-seven? Is your weight under 140 pounds? Are you multilingual? Do you have a college degree?"

After answering "no" to the two last questions, I was sure I would not be selected for an interview.

"May I have your address? You should receive correspondence from us within a week – it will explain all you need to know for your interview. No promises, though, as there are over 10,000 applicants for 1,100 jobs. Do you have any questions?"

I tried to slow my breathing down. I wanted to ask how much they paid, but I thought that might be pushing it. "No thank you,"

With that, she hung up and I geared myself for the fight of my life.

I knew I had to work through the anger and disappointment of my family. Not only had I embarrassed them – unintentionally of course – with the cancellation of my wedding, but now I was leaving a Christian college and on my way to hell by becoming a stewardess.

Defending my decision was a nightly discussion.

"A stewardess serves liquor, you know?" my aunt commented, one night at dinner. "Liquor destroyed your family. I want to be the first to point this out. You're turning your back on God. Think of all that He has done for you."

"I can tell people about God when I serve them the liquor," I argued. "I can be the light in the wilderness."

My sister giggled in the corner, but my aunt gave me the evil eye, my humor lost on her.

My parents had divorced. Then my mother abandoned us, and my father pawned me and my siblings off to my sweet aunt in California while he struggled to pay off his debts in Texas. My aunt was correct in saying that liquor was the reason my parents had fought so violently. There should be a test to determine whether people should be parents. Mine would have flunked.

I had managed to get singing scholarships at a Christian Preparatory school and then again in college. Singing was my aunt's dream, not mine, but I entertained her dreams. Marrying would have released her from this responsibility. I longed to do this, but obviously I had failed.

The college had agreed to reinstate me, if I was interested in returning, but I wasn't interested. Going back to a small, parochial college, with its constant gossip, was nearly as painful as seeing high school friends again. What had once been cool about having a fiancé in Vietnam was now an albatross around my neck.

There were so many signs leading me to TWA: the failed rendezvous with Vince, the stewardess, Anne Marie, and the assaults of the constant TWA advertisements on radio. Could this be God directing me?

CHAPTER FOUR

THE INTERVIEW

While I was in high school, a popular southern Californian pastime was "cruising." I would fill my car with $1 worth of gas – which would last me all night – and then I'd head over to the infamous "Tweedy Boulevard" with my girlfriends twittering in the back. We'd patiently wait for DJ Wolfman Jack to howl as he sang "Hey there, Little Red Riding Hood" over the too-loud radio, and then we'd laugh the night away.

The purpose of all this was to show off my car, while surreptitiously trying to meet boys. I had a 1956 canary-yellow Chevy which was, by all accounts, a boy magnet. The boys were of some interest to me, but I never found them as hard to meet as my friends did. My shyer counterparts used my outgoing personality and good looks as bait.

If the night was still young, and we hadn't been successful in our endeavors, we'd head to Los Angeles International Airport (LAX), hoping to catch some T.V. show participants on their way back to New York. I wasn't as enamored with or enthralled with them as my friends were – my religion didn't even allow me to go to the movies – but I always went along with the adventure.

LAX was not just an airport – it was the airport of Hollywood stars. It was in some ways, a live canvas upon which they could be viewed in their raw, unfiltered states of inebriation. At this late hour, the airport would be alive with long black limousines. Silently, they slithered through the terminals, their contents secreted behind tinted windows. Their drivers, tanned and muscular, wore mirrored sunglasses not unlike those of the California Highway Patrol. We all knew if we were patient, we might get a rare glimpse of a bona fide celebrity.

Hollywood and TWA made a perfect combination for star gazers. TWA entered the jet age in 1959. Many say this happened primarily to fly guests to and from the infamous *Tonight Show*, hosted by Johnny Carson. On occasion, Howard Hughes would commandeer a plane – "his airplane" – without care or concern for passengers waiting to depart. What better way for an owner of an airline to impress a pretty starlet? His employees were left scrambling for alternate flights and creative excuses for the disappearance of the airplane.

As I stood there under a Crew Bus sign, however, I was unaware of the legacy of TWA.

"Are you here for an interview?" a uniformed woman asked. I nodded nervously. She smiled and added, "Good luck."

The TWA bus arrived, unloading pilots and hostesses as I waited my turn to get on. I was encouraged to see their camaraderie – perhaps my life was truly changing in a positive way. There was hope.

As we entered the hangar complex, we drove next to what I would later identify as a Boeing 747. It was massive – its engine, as large as a small house, lay dissembled on the ground. Mechanics, resembling ants, crawled over it.

As soon as the bus stopped, a woman, clipboard in hand, checked my name off and guided me to a large room. She handed me a name badge and told me to be seated.

The room began to fill with young women, each one easily qualifying as a Miss California candidate. I began to question my decision; many were tall and blonde, with perfect makeup – real beach beauties. I was pretty in a Christian college sort of way, but these girls were Hollywood starlets in the making.

I shuffled uneasily in my seat, insecurity now overtaking my previous whiff of courage, preparing to head for the door, when an older woman introduced herself to the group. The doors were then closed, and my escape was denied.

"TWA is hiring," she said. "The 747, the newest member of our fleet, requires 16 hostesses. That's a dramatic increase from the five on our current jets." She went on to explain that 10,000 women nationwide were applying for 1,100 hostess positions.

Each participant was asked to stand and introduce themself. The introductions were pretty carbon-copy, and at the end, the obligatory question was asked: "Why do you want this job?" I answered that my plans to get married had changed. I really wanted to say that I had been dumped at the altar, but that sounded like a pity party and I didn't want that.

After a short break, we were given a questionnaire asking about our job histories. I was sure this would eliminate me from any chance of employment, as my only jobs were with Taco Bell and Sears – and did I mention I quit college?

After handing in our forms, we were told to wait for a letter to schedule the next interview. Honestly, I never expected one, but two weeks later, an envelope embellished with the TWA logo eyed me suspiciously from the kitchen counter. This was either rejection or an invitation to the final interview. Would I be hired? What to do? I knew practically nothing about being a hostess – what was I supposed to wear? What about my hair? It hung comfortably down to my waist, and one of the requirements was short, shoulder length hair. I didn't want to cut my hair, but if this was an invitation, I'd have to deal with it.

As I picked up the envelope, I felt a quickening of my heart. I would either be a candidate for a life of excitement as a TWA hostess, or an unmarried waitress at a dead-end job.

My hands shook as I opened the letter, but I exhaled a short squeal of relief when I realized I had been selected to return for a final interview.

It dawned on me, however, that I knew nothing about the job or TWA. I couldn't just depend on the word of a stranger, even if she was employed by an airline. I then realized that the library, my fount of knowledge, was close by.

As I arrived at the small community library, I immediately recognized the librarian, she was a member of my church. Not wanting to alert her to my new job, I tried finding anything that might be written. After searching unsuccessfully, I had to ask her for help.

"Do you have any books about stewardesses, or maybe TWA air hostesses?" I asked.

She sat upright. "Well let's see. Not much written on *that* profession." She raised her eyebrows, and as she fiddled with the card catalog, she felt inclined to share that stewardesses were just "glorified prostitutes."

"Really?" I asked. "Are you sure?"

"Just read this. It tells you right here." She directed me to the book *Coffee, Tea or Me*, whose back cover boasted the following description: *this huge bestseller, a First-Class jet-age journal, offers a hilarious gold mine of outrageous anecdotes from the high-flying and amorous lives of those busty, lusty, adventuresome young women of the swinging '60s known as stews.*

Well, I wasn't lusty, and definitely not busty. Sitting down to read, I swore softly under my breath. The librarian, with better hearing than I realized, shook her head in agreement. One thing was for sure – this book would need to stay here, far away from my family's prying eyes.

The librarian also steered me to the newspaper section where I browsed news headlines regarding TWA. I learned that TWA and Pan Am were fighting for air supremacy over the Atlantic Ocean, with the 747 as their weapon of choice.

Later, I tackled the hair issue with the help of a Hollywood hair stylist. One small hairpiece called a "fall" transformed my hair into the perfect collar-length style. She also showed me the art of applying false eyelashes. I was ready to nail this job.

The return interview was less intimidating, as I felt like the recruiters had already made their decisions. At my one-on-one interview, I was asked if I was running away from something. My reply was yes, but that it wasn't the police. My interviewer laughed, and I hoped she didn't ask any more personal questions.

After being measured, weighed, and checked over by a doctor, I left the airport still unsure of my fate.

Two weeks later, a package arrived. I was thrilled to read that I was accepted to the academy. Enclosed with the letter was a one-way ticket to Kansas City and a study guide about airplanes.

As I shared this with my family, they seemed genuinely excited for me. Now it seemed, the topic of each dinner touched on Kansas City. The crime statistics and the influence of the Kansas City Mafia were central to my brother's contributions to the discourse. He must also have visited the library – prior to this, I never recalled the 'sunflower state' being a topic of our dinner table.

One week before my departure, my family, as well as those of the other candidates, dined at an upscale restaurant in Marina Del Ray as guests of TWA. The airline wanted to develop a partnership with the families, and the excitement was palpable – "Up, Up, and Away," the theme song of TWA, played in the background as waiters served us lobster and filet mignon. It was the first time that we were informed that it cost $5,000 to train us. It was clear they wanted a return on their hefty investment.

As we left the restaurant, a handsome pilot in uniform, who clearly had enjoyed his wine, bumped into my aunt while staring at me. "Thank you for entrusting your daughter to us. We will take good care of her."

"I'm sure you will," she responded.

The food, the music, and the excitement of a new career left me breathless, and the conversation with my family on the drive home reflected that.

My family had been cleverly seduced into the world of TWA. So had I.

CHAPTER FIVE

RAWHIDE

The morning of my departure for Kansas City was beautiful and sunny. The air, mixed with smog and a hint of the ocean, brought on a feeling of melancholy as my departure approached. This home had given me the safety and comfort that had eluded me in childhood and now I was leaving for an unknown future – was this the right decision?

When my aunt brought us from Texas, I slept on a cot in the living room. Some may have felt deprived, but I felt blessed to be in her warm and loving home. As I stood near my bedroom window, I was reminded of the joy I felt when my aunt announced that I was moving to my own room. We painted it a soft lilac.

The feeling of contentment soon dissipated as the sound of my aunt's cheerful voice greeted me from the kitchen. "Good morning," she said. "This is the day the Lord hath made. Rejoice and be glad."

The trauma that I had endured as a young child had made me an angry young woman, but my aunt insisted that I enter the kitchen with a smile and a cheery "hello" each day. She had an eighth-grade education, but a graduate degree in human philosophy, and this one small act had changed my overall attitude.

After much discussion, she volunteered to take me to the airport. She was enjoying the notoriety from her co-workers at the Boeing plant – not everyone had a niece going to Kansas City to become an "air hostess." Even in her blue-collar world, one could appreciate the celebrity of this glamorous profession.

As we entered the morning traffic, I opened a brochure from TWA and read aloud: "In direct response to the addition of the 747 to our fleet, TWA has commissioned a $10 million training center to be built. Located in Overland Park, Kansas on a pristine plot of 34.4 acres, it will serve as the elite training facility for not only hostesses but other employees as well."

"Well, that sounds pretty exciting," she said. "I pray this is God's plan for you; you really had a future singing for Him."

I knew she was disappointed in me, and I so wanted her to approve of my decision. Luckily, something was about to happen that would seal the deal for me.

After parking the car, we walked toward the terminal. A skycap tipped his hat to me as I handed him my luggage. "It's a banner day for TWA!" he said, dropping my bag on the conveyor belt. "We have a plane full of beautiful girls." He must have recognized my destination, along with the other women going to Kansas City.

As we walked into the airport, a swarm of hysterical women encircled a man who was being escorted towards the departure gates. Airline red-coats edged him closer to the airplane. Tall and handsome, with bright green eyes, he seemed oddly familiar.

My aunt, normally quiet and demure, joined the fray. She shouted in my ear, "It's Rawhide!" Her voice, though strained, was reminiscent of a young fan at a Beatles concert.

There he was: gorgeous Clint Eastwood. He was dressed in a perfectly tailored suit, which paralleled his toned and muscular build, and, as he attempted to get past fans and board his flight, he threw a perfect Hollywood smile their way.

My aunt's eyes sparkled with delight as she scanned the departure board. "He's on your plane!" she announced. "He's going to Kansas City with you! Dianna, please get his autograph and all sins will be forgiven."

Rummaging through her over-sized purse, she retrieved a pen and an old piece of paper. I knew she wasn't serious about forgiving my sins, but I was now determined to repay some of her kindness with this small gesture.

When it was my turn to board, I hugged her. I walked down the jetway and as I turned back to wave goodbye, she gave me her cutest smile and mimicked the act of handwriting.

On the plane, I walked past him, seated snugly in First Class, and lingered longer than necessary, in order to catch his eye. He smiled, and I continued my journey to the coach section.

As the 727 taxied down the runway, I mentally stored my emotions away, reminding myself that this is what I wanted. But tears still welled in my eyes as I saw my beloved ocean disappear underneath the clouds. "I'll be back, my friend," I mumbled.

Making my way to the bathroom, which I now call a lavatory, I was blocked by the beverage cart. The hostess told me to go to first class. Pushing the dividing curtain aside, I found myself staring into the eyes of the legend.

"Well, hello again. How are you little lady?" he said.

"Um, I'm fine, thank you." I slid past him as I made my way to the bathroom.

Damn, damn, damn! Remembering my aunt's request, I retrieved the paper and pen from my purse. Brushing my hair, I engaged my courage.

When I left the lavatory, I saw he was seated again, but he looked up and gave me another smile. Mustering my best grin, I stopped at his seat.

Bending over, I whispered, "My aunt dearly loves you. Would you be so kind as to give me your autograph?"

As he reached over to take the pen and paper from me, a voice came from behind: "What are you doing up here?"

The First-Class hostess stood close, her feathers ruffled and beak ready for pecking as she protected her brood, but before I could defend myself, he interrupted her. "Why, I invited her to come and get this autograph for Aunt…"

"Vertele," I added.

The hostess relaxed. "That's fine," she said, and clucked back to her work.

"How do you spell Vertele?"

As I spelled it for him, I realized that I was embarrassed that her name wasn't Gladys or Sophie.

"This is an old German name," he said, probably just trying to make me feel better.

As he handed me the paper, he asked, "Are you one of the trainees?"

"Yes."

He whispered "Well, when you graduate, try to be a little more subtle than her with the fans. I actually like them," he chuckled.

I placed the precious paper in my purse as I quickly returned to my seat, fearing more wrath from the hostess.

During the flight, I concentrated on the hostesses. They were kind and efficient, keeping the passengers engaged in conversation as they served the meals. I wondered how I could do this job with such grace – surely the academy would teach me all I needed to know?

After a couple of hours, I could feel the plane descend. I strained my eyes to make out my temporary home.

The landscape did not resemble California in any way – it was completely brown, void of anything green. Large parcels of land were partitioned with farmhouses and barns, and with what looked like cattle spread across the fields.

As we descended, a haze from nearby smokestacks clouded the view of ramshackle houses near the freeway. Train tracks resembling a large spider web appeared next to hundreds of stock pens. My brother was right: Kansas City was a cow town. And it looked cold.

"Ladies and gentlemen, Welcome to Kansas City, home of TWA. The time is 2:09 P.M. and the temperature is 32 degrees. You may have noticed the lovely ladies on our flight today. They are on their way to becoming TWA Hostesses. Join me in welcoming them to their new home."

As I stood at the front door waiting for my turn to deplane, the hostess from first class whispered from behind me, "Don't ever pull that stunt again on my airplane."

"I won't." As I responded I thought, *Next time it will be my airplane.*

As we walked to the bus, a limousine cruised close by. As my new best friend turned to enter his limo, he looked up and waved at me. I recalled the autograph stowed deep inside my purse, and I waved back, in awe of my good luck.

My first day was one of the most exciting days of my career, and it would mark the beginning of more exciting and memorable days to come.

CHAPTER SIX

KANSAS CITY HERE I COME!

The Kansas City Airport was a collection of small compact buildings, much like the Quonset huts my father had lived in while stationed in Alaska. It was dedicated as New Richards Field in 1927 by Charles Lindbergh, who mapped Transcontinental Air Transports' cross-country routes before its merger with Western Air to form TWA. He piloted the Lindbergh Line – christened by Amelia Earhart – from Los Angeles to New York in record time.

Kansas City was designated as the headquarters of TWA after its corporate offices moved there from New York. That day passengers dressed in their finest, lining up to board a TWA jet as children clung to their mothers, their small faces peeking around at the scary airplanes. With no jetways, passengers were assailed with the sights and sounds of an active and vibrant airport.

As I waited for my turn to board the red and white TWA bus, the smell of freshly brewed coffee overrode the aroma of jet fuel. I later learned that the Folgers Coffee Company was located one mile from the airport.

When the last trainee sat down, the bus jolted to a start. A few of us jumped as the driver bellowed loudly, "Welcome to Kansas City!" He maneuvered the large bus through the airport onto the Broadway Bridge, which would lead us to the Breech Training Academy in Kansas.

The downtown area reflected a long-ago lifestyle. Older buildings were carved with ornate facades, reminiscent of the rich clientele of the past – my brother had regaled me with stories of the Kansas City Mafia sharing their wealth by opening restaurants, often with Italian themes. The streets were clean, with large glass store fronts announcing new fashion trends and advertisements of $5 dinners. There were no cattle roaming the streets, as had been predicted by my friends.

We passed through Mission Hills, Kansas, where many of the richest residents lived. Their homes rivaled even the homes in Hollywood – large lawns resembling golf courses were filled with fountains and immense, landscaped flower beds. As we entered each small community larger fountains complemented the roundabouts.

"Okay listen up ladies," the drivers said, "I've been doing this so much this week my voice is getting as horse as a bullfrog during dating season." A few giggles from the front made him smile. "You gals in the back will have to listen. I know y'all have read lots about the academy, but I'd like to give you the real scoop. I'm not only a driver – I'm also a security guard – and it's not all fun and games here."

The driver went on to explain that the complex was surrounded by wired fences and high walled cement blocks, designed to "keep the young men out and the young women in.

"Apparently, before their training was up, some girls wanted to go home, or they thought they had fallen in love with one of the locals."

"We'd prefer you just tell us rather than trying to leave on your own, if you get my drift," the driver said. "The local men fancy finding themselves a sweetheart amongst you beauties, and it's our job to protect you from them until you graduate. There are lots of rules here – if you are serious about this job, don't break any of them, or they will send you home."

Thinking back to the TWA dinner party before I left home. As my brother dipped his lobster tail into warmed butter, I had the distinct impression that he would snitch me off in a heartbeat if I contemplated going AWOL.

The bus made a sweeping turn into a short driveway, passing a small guardhouse and slowed as the guard tipped his hat. A long concrete walkway was covered with a lattice and encrusted with honeysuckle vines, dormant now - I imagined they'd be impressive in the summer.

As the brakes groaned, the door opened and an older woman boarded. She smiled as she gazed down the aisles.

"Good afternoon, ladies. I'd like to be the first to welcome you to the Breech Training Academy; I am the director here. My name is Mrs. Boylan. If you would, please gather your personal belongings and form a line. We will process you and get you on your way to lunch. You must be famished!"

The line moved quickly. As our meager luggage was tagged to be delivered to our living quarters, we were each given a room key.

When we entered the cafeteria, which was large and drenched with sunlight, we were stopped by an older woman with a clipboard. She asked our names and instructed us to step on a scale.

"The scale will tell the tale. " A voice from behind me whispered.

The woman reminded us that we could be weighed daily, and sometimes without warning. I wasn't worried, but I saw a few girls who might be.

Soft music serenaded us as we lined up for lunch, and chefs with traditional toques stood at attention, waiting for our requests.

I limited myself to a tuna sandwich and a Coke. As I sat down at an already occupied table, I saw that one girl had loaded her plate with spaghetti and meatballs, surrounded by garlic bread.

"This place is really cool," she said, stuffing a large meatball into her mouth. "I can't believe they've already begun to weigh us."

I was mesmerized at her ability to talk while she chewed. "I was just two pounds under the limit," she said, "and the lady that hired me warned me about gaining weight. She said if I gain, I'm out!"

"Gain how much?" a brunette candidate asked.

"She said any, like more than I am now or will be later." She laughed as another meatball dripped on her fork.

Her name was Mandy McCree, and I could easily see how the recruiters decided to hire her. Her face was cherubic, and her blonde hair and dimples finished off the perfect combination of the California girl.

The conversation drifted into boyfriends and hometowns. At the table was a redhaired girl named Rebecca, or Becky as she preferred. She was from Kansas, and she told us that she was just waiting on her boyfriend to finish college so they could tie the knot. I was somewhat jealous of her wedding plans. I kept my past quiet, not willing to engage.

After a while, I noticed Mrs. Boylan appear at the door with a uniformed woman.

"Hello, everyone, I am Lucy Beaverton, one of the many training instructors here. When I call your name, please follow me. I will be your home room instructor, and I would like to take you on a short tour of the facility. After the tour, you will have the rest of the day to unpack before we meet again prior to dinner. Classes start tomorrow at 8:45 AM.

She called the names of 20 women, including mine, as other instructors assembled groups all around the cafeteria.

"I will begin the tour here. This is your cafeteria; you will eat here daily. It is open from 6 A.M. to 6 P.M., and the chefs are here at breakfast, lunch, and dinnertime. There will be a selection of hot meals prepared daily in addition to salads and sandwiches. I will remind you that if your weight is something you were warned about, you should be careful. Weight gain will get you sent home. Your weight may be recorded daily."

As she led us out of the cafeteria, she explained that the complex we were in was the largest training facility of its kind in the world. It housed 32 octagonal classrooms and 10 galley trainers, which are representations of the many aircraft cabins in the TWA fleet. On the second floor there were also grooming rooms, where makeup and poise would be taught.

A very wide stairway led to the rooms on the second floor. As we began to ascend the steps, she said, "Before you leave this facility, you will accomplish walking up and down these stairs with perfect poise and confidence. It sounds silly now, but I can assure you that you will learn how to do this."

She also told us that each of us would be meeting with a makeup and hair consultant. If a hair cut or coloring was needed, it would be done right here on the premises.

Next, we stopped in front of a small storefront. "This is the Lancôme sales office," she explained. "All of your makeup, cremes, and nail polish can be purchased at this Lancôme counter, where you will get an airline discount. They have some very odd business hours, which are posted daily on the door."

We walked down a glass hallway with doors on one side. "These are our training rooms," she said. "You will spend every day here for the next five weeks, except Saturday and Sunday, though sometimes we may add additional training on the weekends for classes or students who are struggling with the curriculum. Our classes work as a team, and you will be scored as a team. Teamwork is essential when working a flight, and we hope it flourishes here as well."

Inside the room a large screen filled one wall and a podium sat to one side. There was also a strange-looking desk.

Sensing our curiosity she said "This is the first of its kind in classroom technology. It features a single horseshoe-shaped desk – you will notice that each desk allows for ten students to sit at once all having a front row seat."

Three buttons sat to the right of each seat, and she explained that these buttons would allow each student to respond to impromptu tests given daily by the instructors, quickly and privately. These tests would help the instructor judge the individual progress of each student.

The answers were recorded on the teacher's panel and right and wrong lights flashed at each trainee's desk. Each position had an attached chair that swung out – they looked uncomfortable.

"Do not be late to class," she said. "I am sure you have heard this repeatedly, but tardiness has no place in this industry and will not be tolerated. Think of it this way: a late hostess could delay or possibly cause a flight to be canceled, so a late hostess could be terminated."

"You will be tested after each class. In the first week we will give you a break. You need to know that a test score under 90 is considered problematic. After that first week, you are on your own. Training manuals have been delivered to your rooms. I would suggest that you all look over the material tonight."

As she led us back to the buildings entrance, she said she had one more thing to tell us: "Leaving the compound on unsupervised trips, gaining weight, and being disrespectful to a superior are just a few things that could end your new profession and lead to a quick trip back home. You might occasionally hear of a trainee being sent home, but most often it has more to do with personal problems than disciplinary problems."

We filed out of the main building and into the open air. The instructor pointed to a long, winding concrete path that led past an octagonal building and finally ended at a group of apartments. She explained that this would be the path we would walk to class each morning.

We walked over to the octagonal building and then went inside. We saw a very large swimming pool. *Things are looking up*, I thought.

"This is used to train International Hostesses for a water ditching. You are allowed in here anytime, if a class is not in progress."

We then walked to the apartments. At the apartments, she explained that these were our residence halls. Each studio holds 10 rooms that we would share with another trainee. There are three residence halls, and we would be training with our wing of 20 girls. When we graduated and were assigned to our domiciles, we would do so at the same time."

"What is a domicile?" a voice asked from the back of the group.

"A domicile is a home base. It's where you will live," the instructor replied. "After you have completed your probationary period of six months, you can request a transfer to another domicile."

Our wing was a sunken living room with a large television and study area and several comfy looking couches. Each living area had a different motif designed around the Mediterranean, the Far East, Africa, England, or France. Ours was French, the walls covered with pictures of the Eiffel Tower and Notre Dame.

"Ladies, this will be your residence for five short weeks. We expect you all to live here with respect for each other's privacy and safety. Treat each other as you would a family member. We do not expect you to lock your doors, but we also do not expect any theft. It will be prosecuted, and the thief will be ejected from the academy."

We were now allowed to find our rooms and unpack our suitcases. There were folders in our rooms that we were responsible to open and read through to familiarize ourselves with Kansas City and the rules and regulations of the academy. The rest of the day would be ours. Dinner would be served promptly at 6:00 P.M."

When I got to my room, I saw it was already occupied by a blonde, blue-eyed woman in the process of unpacking her bag.

"Hi, my name is Angela," she said, reaching her hand out with a friendly smile and an accent that I was unfamiliar with.

"I'm Dianna. Where are you from?"

"Connecticut, and you?"

"L.A."

"Which side of the room do you want?" she asked.

I told her I didn't care, so she said she'd take the one next to the bathroom, since she was a smoker. She promised not to smoke in the room.

Great, a smoker, I thought. I hated cigarette smoke, but this wasn't the time to make an enemy.

As we unpacked, she told me that she was 27 and was a little worried about passing all the tests. When I asked why, she said it was because it had been a long time since she attended school.

"So how about you? Are you worried?" she asked.

"No," I said. "I'm excited."

"How old are you?"

"Twenty. I'll be 21 in August."

She smiled. "That explains it then.".

"Explains what?"

"Your enthusiasm."

CHAPTER SEVEN

BREECH TRAINING ACADEMY

The first class of my airline career was a TWA history class. We learned that Western Air Express made its debut in Los Angeles on July 23, 1925, and that after doing well on its own, in 1930 it merged with another airline named Transcontinental Air Transport. The new company became Transcontinental and Western Air (TWA), and in 1950, with world expansion on their minds, the company officially changed its name to Trans World Airlines.

In 1929, TWA was the first airline to offer coast-to-coast travel with a combination of air and rail service, a trip that took 48 hours. TWA was the first to have flight plans, flight logs, and cockpit checklists, thanks to the intervention of Charles Lindbergh, who after flying across the Atlantic, worked on TWA's technical team. He designed air routes, runways, hired pilots and checked on the safety of the airplanes that they flew.

TWA was also the first to organize a weather department, develop a two-way radio telephone system, and inaugurate cargo service – and this was all before 1932.

TWA had spent its formative years working on airline safety. Around 1950, the customer service aspects came into play. They developed the quick-frozen, pre-cooked method of food preparation so that passengers could enjoy a hot meal. They also developed a way to freshly brew coffee as they flew the first nonstop international flight to Rome in 1957. Finally, they showed the first in-flight movie in 1961 – "By Love Possessed" with Lana Turner.

Our instructor – an older woman, was unlike the young men and women we had seen on campus. Her dress was conservative. She wore her hair in a tight bun with glasses perched on her large nose. I felt akin to her in some way. She reminded me of the ladies from my church.

"Have you ever flown with Howard Hughes?" someone asked.

"No," the instructor replied bluntly. "I will give him credit for fighting the good fight with Congress after World War Two so that we could fly across the ocean and compete with Pan Am. He proved he was a good lawyer, but not such a great owner."

She didn't appear to want to say more, and no other hands appeared.

The history class ended, and the instructor allowed us a 15-minute break. When we returned, we took our first test, which was a breeze – so far, I liked this whole idea.

The next instructor was a male – a pilot with a receding hairline. He wasn't as handsome as we had been led to believe all the pilots were.

"Good morning, ladies. My name is Fred," he said.

I had already decided that he had to be a little weird – pilots wouldn't want to spend their time teaching a bunch of 20-year-olds about airplanes.

He began his lesson with a staggering statement: "TWA flies five types of airplanes, and before you graduate in five weeks, you will have learned the locations of all the emergency exits and equipment on every plane, uses for that equipment, how to operate that equipment, and lots of other fun stuff."

He smiled and then he laughed. Some in the class giggled.

"Oh, and yes, I forgot – you will learn how to jump out of a burning airplane, and hopefully take some passengers with you."

The class became quieter. In 1931, TWA nearly went out of business after Flight 599 crashed near Bazaar, Kansas on March 31, killing all eight on board the plane, including University of Notre Dame coach Knute Rockne. Carole Lombard was returning from a war bonds rally in Indianapolis when her Los Angeles TWA Sky Sleeper crashed over Nevada on January 17, 1942.

"We are under a magnifying glass each time a crash happens," Fred said. "We study the causes, make changes, and hopefully correct the mistakes. The FAA and National Transportation Safety Board are tasked with the job of improving air safety."

The class remained silent as he continued: "As you progress in this course, and as you grow to become a seasoned airline employee, keep one thing in mind regarding safety: every rule that is established has a case history of death or pain attached to it. The memos usually follow the disaster, and the rules follow the memos. Trust me, someday you will understand."

No one laughed this time. He explained that this class was designed to help us learn not only the process, but the procedures to place safety on our side, thus ensuring a safe airline for ourselves and the passengers.

After a moment or two, the room went black. A movie began, showing a series of scenes depicting the aftermath of airplane crashes. The scenes were graphic – they depicted burned-out shells of destroyed airplanes from all over the world, a brutal reminder of how dangerous air travel could be. The room was quiet when the lights came on.

"My job today, and for the next five weeks, is to help you understand that your primary job at TWA is to save the lives of your passengers. It could be the unexpected and unplanned crash of an airplane, a decompression, or the death or illness of a passenger. These situations happen – you will be the person who doesn't panic. You will be trained to think instinctively. You will save lives, if necessary, and you will live through it."

I hoped I would be able to react positively in an emergency. I felt faint thinking of the crash scenes. What had I done to myself?

He explained that the scenes we just witnessed were those of aircraft disasters. Some of them were caused by weather, some by pilot error, and some were still under investigation – we would study each one of them, and each year we would return there and study each subsequent disaster to re-qualify for another year of flight. Our pilots were required to do the same thing – it was called an AER, or Annual Emergency Review."

"We hope that by studying these scenarios you can learn," Fred said. "Have you heard the saying, 'Those who cannot remember the past are condemned to repeat it?' This comes from the writings of George Santayana. We remember our past and every other airline's past, too. It's our way of hopefully steering clear of future accidents."

Aside from being pretty and self-confident, he explained that we must also be knowledgeable and well-trained. The lives of our passengers depended on our ability to learn this material.

We learned that we would be studying each of the five airplanes that were currently in our fleet: the Douglas DC9, the Convair 880, the Boeing 727, the Boeing 707, and – the newest and most exciting – the Boeing 747. Each of these aircraft had emergency door exits and window exits, and we would be studying how to arm them, open them, and exit them for maximum safety. We would also be learning the uses of emergency oxygen and the basics of first aid.

"An airplane cannot always land in time if a passenger needs care," Fred said. "Television loves to portray emergencies that end with a doctor on board, but real life just isn't like that. First, doctors aren't always willing to help, even if they are on board. They are fearful of lawsuits that might result from a patient not approving of the outcome. And secondly, what if there isn't a doctor on board? Then you must provide the needed aid until the aircraft is on the ground."

We all recognized the importance of this curriculum. As he began to dismiss class, we were encouraged to take the manuals he handed out. Each one covered each of the five jets we'd be studying.

As we were departing, he offered a few final words: "When an airplane is in trouble and the lives of the passengers are at risk, you are the only lifeline. You must remember that your courage will save lives."

CHAPTER EIGHT

DINING SERVICE TRAINING

Dining Service Training was held in the actual shell of an airplane. The tubular structure was painted white, with the TWA logo emblazoned on the side. As we lined up to enter the classroom, which was called a "mock-up," it was surreal – I felt as if we were boarding an airplane.

Inside, we were invited to view the galley. It was small, compact, and filled with ovens on the top and steel containers on the bottom.

Our trainer, a diminutive young man, stood silently, watching as we sat in the real airplane seats that lined the inside. "Guten Morgen, Ladies," he said. "My name is Wolfgang and as you can tell from my accent, I am from Vienna. I will be your dining instructor for the next five weeks. My real job is as a purser on international flights. Now, let's begin."

I settled into my seat and looked around – the other trainees looked just as excited as I was.

"There are two things that help a potential businessman make his choice for air travel," Wolfgang said. "Can you guess what they are?"

One girl held up her hand. "Us?" she giggled.

"No, sorry. Every airline hires pretty girls."

Another hand waved. "The price?"

"No. What if I told you that all ticket prices are the same? A group of men called the CAB regulate the ticket prices and dole out the airline routes like candy."

When no other suggestions were made, he stepped toward us. "How about the food?" he suggested. "Today we will begin to teach you how to cook and serve the delicious meals that our international chefs prepare daily. Does anyone know how to cook a perfect chateaubriand? Has anyone eaten beluga caviar?"

Mandy, our new class gourmand, raised her hand. "Isn't caviar just dressed-up fish eggs?

"No, my dear. After this class, you will never again refer to caviar as fish eggs."

I was beginning to get excited. My knowledge of food consisted of menus derived from a well-worn Betty Crocker cookbook. These things that he spoke of were some I had never dreamed of tasting, let alone cooking and serving. Was I really going to eat fish eggs?

Seemingly flustered, he walked closer to us. "A quick lesson. You must never refer to yourselves as stewardesses – you are 'air hostesses.' We invite the passenger into our homes, and we serve him graciously. Comprenez-vous?" He smiled. "Oh, that is 'do you understand,' in French. You are in the French apartment, yes?"

We all laughed. It was cool that he had done his homework and knew that our apartment was in the French motif.

He walked down the aisle handing us each a menu.

"TWA is known worldwide for its food, and when this course is over, you will understand why. This is a coach menu from a transcontinental flight, like LAX to JFK. We always offer a choice of three meals. Please take a moment and read though the menu."

I held my hand up and asked, "Sir, will be cooking or warming the meals?"

"Great question. Your name?"

"It's Dianna."

"Dianna, our entrees are chilled with dry ice. They are warmed to a temperature of 350 degrees. Our new convection ovens take care of the guess work – set them at 350 degrees for 30 minutes and voila – they are done. However, we cook our chateaubriand from a raw state; it is cooked to the customers preference.

An audible groan filled the room, and he held up both his hands. "That's not the first time I've heard this. It's rare that a trainee will ever touch a first-class galley – it is a very senior position. By the time you are senior enough to work a first-class galley you will have learned how to cook these magnificent cuts of meat."

Wolfgang went on to tell us that the type of meal service we would be serving would depend on the time of day that the flight departed and on the length of that flight, in addition to what our competitors were doing. TWA employed what were known as 'Sky Spies' – all the airlines did this. "They spy on us, and we spy on them," Wolfgang said.

He handed us each a manual that described the domestic food and liquor service in detail. He suggested that we start memorizing the wine and liquor selections, emphasizing that we only serve the best brand names on all flights. It's not enough to give a passenger vodka and tonic, he told us, we must say Smirnoff vodka and tonic when we serve it. TWA has an agreement with their vendors that we would consistently use their names when making a presentation, something that would be tested repeatedly.

He asked if there were any questions. One woman raised her hand. "Do we serve liquor to just anyone? Or do we ask for identification? What if they won't give it to us?"

"Well, don't we have a lot of questions on our first day?" He girlishly waved his hand. "You must never knowingly serve liquor to anyone under 21. You may ask for their I.D. and if they refuse to give it to you, then you don't serve them; it's as basic as that. We are under international law when our planes are at altitude, but we are governed by domestic guidelines."

I was wondering if I would have been carded on my flight from Los

Angeles if I'd asked for a cocktail. I was only 20 years old. Behind me, Angela chortled. "I've been drinking on airplanes since I was 16. Never been carded, ever."

Overhearing her, Wolfgang smiled. "Lucky you. I hope you pay attention on your own flights – it's against FAA rules to allow a passenger under 21 to drink, and it's also your job to serve each passenger a maximum of two drinks per flight."

"How will we know if they're getting drunk?" someone asked.

"It's your job to keep that tallied up on drinkers. Count the liquor bottles on their tray, if necessary. But keep a sharp eye out."

"What if they bring their own liquor on board?"

"Then you tell them to hand it over. Let them know you will mix their drinks, otherwise they can't have it back. But I would suggest this situation will be handled by your senior hostess."

The day ended with the class rehearsing the pronunciation of the wine gewurztraminer – it was quite a mouthful.

We ended up really enjoying the class, serving each other meals cooked in convection ovens. We also learned about the new microwave ovens which were loaded on the 747s – cooking in two minutes instead of 30 was quite exciting.

As we walked to the sunken living room in our apartment, we found a couple of our classmates watching T.V. On it, a pilot from TWA was speaking to a newsman in New York. It seems that a group called PATCO, the Professional Air Traffic Controllers Organization, was staging a "slowdown" at all the major airports. Angela explained that PATCO was a union that represented the guys who controlled the airplanes in the air – she knew this because her cousin was an air controller in New York.

The pilot said that the controllers were "working by the book," which was causing major delays. He said his plane had sat on the runway for two hours for no obvious reason, that he had to return to the gate and get more fuel. He was very insistent that this was all getting out of control: "The government needs to get involved, otherwise passengers are going to catch the brunt of this union problem."

"We'll have to ask the training instructors about that tomorrow," someone said. "This may affect our jobs."

Angela and I left the discussion and returned to our room.

"Do you think we will be fired over this? I asked.

"No idea. 'Ours is not to reason why', my friend. This is out of our control. Let's concentrate on this dining manual."

Dinner became the place for discussions. The weight issue was forever the major topic of conversation. In the first week, everyone was eager to try all the new selections of food, but as time wore on, and the scales became the enemy, bulimia was introduced as a topic.

I was appalled at the description of the process of bulimia – what some women would do to keep this job!

Monday through Friday was devoted to TWA. The weekends were ours, with one exception: if your class was failing, you were not allowed off campus. That group of women had to work over the weekend to raise their grades.

One weekend, we boarded an airplane to experience a "fright flight," where a Boeing 707 was flown around for two hours at many different altitudes and attitudes. Each trainee was handed a barf bag as they sat down and strapped in. The pilots jovially announced, "Okay, this is a Dutch roll" or "here's a touch and go" and we all held on for dear life, trying not to toss our cookies.

The five weeks passed quickly. We studied airplane configurations, emergency procedures, first aid, and cabin service. We also spent a day learning how to stand in public, how to walk like a lady, and how to apply makeup. The public was always watching. We were TWA's billboards.

The grooming class could have been my downfall had it not been for my Hollywood hair secret; I was passed up for a haircut and color. My waist-length hair was covered each day – only my roommate was aware of my deceit.

Other women weren't as lucky – some brunettes became blondes; some redheads became brunettes. Becky, a natural redhead from Kansas promptly threatened to quit if anyone touched her hair with hair dye.

We sat in cabin trainers daily, and watched as our classmates stumbled down the aisles trying to balance heavy trays loaded with porcelain dinnerware that was filled with freshly cooked food. The trays were heavy, the aisles were narrow, and I couldn't imagine doing this in turbulence.

For hours we studied cart presentations for the eight-course menu, memorizing the proper pronunciation of words like Chateaubriand Roti and Coquilles St Jacques.

In the end, as promised on our first day, we all managed to walk down the stairs without looking.

We participated in role playing – while seated on the mock-up aircraft, the instructors handed out personality characteristics to each of us. Some of us played disabled passengers, or mothers with babies attempting to sit in the exit row. We played blind and deaf and "no speaka the English." It was fun, but stressful knowing we were being graded by the instructors.

Occasionally, and without warning, the cabin lights would be dimmed and an evacuation alarm would be initiated. Real and very convincing sounds of screaming passengers would accompany the unnerving sounds of a crash. Window exits would be jammed, while smoke would fill the cabin. The instructors, seated behind one-way glass, graded each student on their performance and knowledge of company procedures. I was so excited to evacuate an airplane that I nearly knocked out one of my classmates with the wing exit. Fortunately, she wasn't injured, and I received a thumbs up.

I would go to bed at night with the sound of the "Emergency Evacuation Alarm" bouncing around in my subconscious.

The hardest part came in the fifth week, when we were tested by the FAA. We were quizzed on everything remotely relating to safety on all five airplanes. We were required to know the location of all emergency equipment on each one, and we were required to know how to arm and disarm our doors, which contained emergency slides.

Because they were all Boeing designs, most of the answers were similar. The exception was the behemoth 747 – the door was so heavy that we needed a power assist mechanism to help us in an emergency. The door's preflight was confusing. We had to look for the "absence of the red ball." That one phrase caused many conversations. Finally, we understood that if the red ball could be seen, that we needed to call a mechanic.

We were prepared for the scariest parts of our jobs daily, so that the final test of jumping into a cabin door slide wasn't as bad as we anticipated. We proudly wore our uniforms during the last week of training, giving our instructors a chance to fix any styling issues.

The week before, we had received our domicile assignments – our entire class was going to New York. We would be flying out of Kennedy, LaGuardia, and Newark. We pretty much knew that New York would be our assigned domicile; that's where the 747 was based. I was prepared to take on the "jumbo," and it thrilled me to know I was going to fly the largest commercial jet in the world.

CHAPTER NINE

GRADUATION

The Boeing 727 drifted easily over the East River between the tallest buildings I had ever seen. *So, this is New York City?* I whispered to myself.

The jet slowed, descending between dark-colored buildings. Thousands of windowpanes reflected in the setting sun, and interminable lines of cars snaked through the streets, commuters making their way home.

My God, how many people live down there? I thought LA traffic was bad!

As we taxied into the gate, one of the girls sang from the back of the plane: "New York, New York, what a wonderful town! The Bronx is up and the Battery's down!"

It was April 17, 1970. Only hours earlier, I had graduated from the academy. I wanted to be excited about coming to New York, but instead, as I looked out of my window, I was overcome with dread.

My home, one of sunny beaches and tanned bodies, would now be replaced by cold gray concrete and icy stares of the locals. Angela, my academy roommate, had warned me about New Yorkers: "They are always in a rush, and they never smile unless they know you – but when they do know you, they're your friend for life."

My thoughts were interrupted by Becky: "We're not in Kansas anymore," she said.

After landing and departing the plane, we all gathered near a woman we learned was an airline supervisor named Ms. Riccolli. She was holding a sign that read "TWA Graduates." Tall, and exquisitely dressed, she herded us to the baggage claim area, and while we waited for our luggage, she handed us each a large packet.

She spoke with a rich New York accent. "The packet I have just handed you is important and will assist you in becoming familiar with your new home."

We each began to flip through the packet.

"There are some very important phone numbers that you might need in an emergency," she continued. "One in particular is the SOD, which is the 'Supervisor on Duty' at JFK. Someone is there to assist you, so call if you get into any trouble or have a question."

Slowly our bags made their way down the carousel, and one by one we heaved our suitcases off. TWA had given each of us a white Samsonite suitcase that was part of our uniform complement. In addition, we had our personal suitcase that we had brought from home, and some of the girls had boxes that contained additional clothing that was purchased in Kansas City.

"I know you are tired and probably somewhat excited," she said. "There is a bus outside waiting to transport you to your temporary home. Collect your luggage and meet me out there – I'll be around until the bus leaves."

As we dragged our overstuffed bags to the bus, a driver directed a younger man, who resentfully stacked them inside the bus undercarriage. He never looked up, even when we attempted a "thank you."

"Well, are you ready? Becky asked.

We approached the door of the bus. "Ready for what?" I responded.

"To experience New York!"

I laughed. "Yep, let's go and experience."

When the last girl boarded, the supervisor appeared at the bus door. "This bus will deliver you all to 48th and Lexington in Manhattan. Your rooms at the Lexington Hotel are paid for by TWA for three days. After that you will be charged a room rate of $25 per day."

A loud groan could be heard throughout the bus. She sighed and continued: "Now girls, we have a service that will help you locate a place to live. Tomorrow morning, you will be expected at JFK Hangar 12 at 10:00 A.M. The directions to the hangar are in your packet – read them entirely and follow them to the letter. No cheating! See you tomorrow."

Cheating? What is she talking about? I thought, rummaging through my pack.

"Forget it – it's too dark to read in here. I've already tried," Angela's said from behind me.

"Take care of our little bunny rabbits, Clyde," the supervisor said as she descended from the bus. She waved goodbye as she disappeared into the crowd.

Seconds later a tall, gorgeous man stuck his head in the bus. "Queens?" he asked.

"No, hostesses!" a graduate shouted from the back of the bus.

The driver turned around in his seat, shooting an annoyed look into the darkened bus. The man took a step closer to the driver, who then placed his hand out like a traffic cop to stop the man from boarding. "This is a charter, buddy, can't you read?"

The man smiled. "Sorry, guess I was daydreaming."

"Come on Clyde, let him ride!" a voice from the back joked.

But the man looked back at us, blew a kiss, and slowly backed out of the bus.

After an uneasy silence, one of the girls asked Clyde, "Did he think we were all queens, like beauty queens?"

Clyde snorted. "Queens? No, girlie. Queens is a borough in New York – you know, like a city within a city? That guy was asking if the bus goes to Queens. Actually, he was probably just hoping to get a free ride with you good-looking dames."

We all watched as the handsome man waved down a cab. The bus driver smiled at our sweet ignorance and started to drive.

I was mesmerized by the cacophony of sounds. In L.A., we were forbidden to sound our horns except in dire emergencies, but horns seemed to be a common form of communication among New Yorkers. Peering through my window, I surmised that pedestrians were moving targets, compared to California, where cars actually stopped for them to cross the road.

As soon as the bus had slowed to the pace of the commuter traffic, Clyde spoke: "Okay, ladies, listen up. I have some important pointers from the standpoint of a native New Yorker. You've got to plan your paths before you walk into the streets. You'll get run over if you stand still, so don't."

"Don't what?" a girl asked.

He smiled into the rearview mirror. "Don't stand still. We got a saying in New York: 'You can tell an out-of-towner by the bird shit on their clothes and the dog shit on their feet.' 'Scuse my language."

"What's that mean, Clyde?" someone asked.

He smiled. "I was hoping you'd ask. Well, you see, out-of-towners are always looking up at the tall buildings, so they never see the dogshit they're walking into, and the pigeons use them for target practice."

He laughed and so did we. "The bad part is, they also target themselves for muggers. So, look the part; walk fast, look straight ahead, and don't stop in the middle of a crowd. Otherwise, you might as well put a sign on your forehead that says, 'mug me.'"

As the traffic merged into the Lincoln Tunnel, the bus slowed again. I have always been a little claustrophobic, which only enhanced Clyde's speech about the construction of the tunnel. He went to great lengths to describe the design, tonnage per square inch of water, and the amount of concrete used.

"The mafia was a little miffed when they had to pay more for their 'concrete overshoes' during this time," he said. When no one responded, he explained that the mafia was known for dumping rivals in the East River covered in concrete, so they'd sink to the bottom.

"Why would they do that?" the same, obviously naïve, girl asked.

"Oh, never mind," Clyde said.

Four traffic lanes turned into one as the bus squeezed into the long line of cabs and commuters. The horns continued to serenade the night. After what seemed like an eternity, we pulled up next to the Lexington Hotel. It appeared small and quaint, its three stories nestled next to much taller buildings.

A short, balding man approached us. "Welcome, welcome to New York, ladies!" he said. "My name is Mario, and I am the concierge of the hotel." He obviously enjoyed his meals, since his last one had left traces on his prominent stomach.

"Don't worry about your luggage; just go to the reception desk," he said. "Your rooms have already been assigned, so just sign your name."

He gazed at the rows of radiant faces – all-American girls, and virginal, or at least they appeared to be. Our new jobs were quite a contrast to those of the ladies who stood at either end of the block, preparing for their nights of work.

Angela and I managed to become roommates once again. Soon we found ourselves walking down a long, dark hallway toward our room. Once we got there, we struggled with the ancient room key.

The rooms were very small, and the beds quite lumpy. The class before us had reported that a malodorous smell had greeted them at the door to their room, where they later found a dead man underneath one of their beds. Fortunately, our room only smelled of mold and Lysol.

I felt a twinge of homesickness for the academy. I had become accustomed to the surroundings, so warm and safe, and the redundancy of the day-to-day life there. I even missed the old guards who had made our business their business.

I hoped New York would grow on me. But for now, I was busy looking underneath my bed, just in case.

CHAPTER TEN

FURLOUGHED ON THE FIRST DAY

Angela was thrilled to be back on the east coast, where Manhattan was a cocktail and not a Kansas college town. During a weekend at Breech Academy, she had asked a cab driver to take her to get a Manhattan. Between her East Coast accent and his poor hearing, he was well on his way to Manhattan, Kansas – a three-hour drive – before she realized her mistake.

After some discussion, he stopped at a Howard Johnson restaurant. She was hoping for a resolution to her quest, but the workers there had no idea what she was talking about. So, she returned to the academy, heartsick and convinced that all Midwesterners were ignorant and misguided – "especially cab drivers."

After we settled into our hotel rooms, Angela loudly insisted on celebrating, alone if necessary: "I'm going out drinking. Anyone with me?"

Down the lonely hall of the hotel, a few doors opened, but no one took her up on her offer. Unphased, she left, humming happily to herself.

I felt sorry for Angela. I knew she was recently divorced, and I imagined that she was lonely for her Connecticut friends. She had related how often she met with them for "drinks and darts."

Around 3:00 in the morning, I heard the door open. She whispered, "I'm home, Mom," and then flopped onto her bed, reeking of liquor and cigar smoke.

I didn't say anything. I hadn't been able to sleep – I had imagined Angela all alone on the street, being mugged, or worse, raped. I had yet to learn that just as Frank Sinatra sang, New York is a city that never sleeps – I soon discovered that the bars close at 3:00 A.M., so that is a perfectly good time to go home.

When our wake-up call came at 6:00 A.M., she moaned and rolled over.

I whispered, "I'm taking a shower – you'd better do the same. We're leaving here at 8:30 for our date with TWA. Breakfast is downstairs in an hour."

At breakfast, as we prepared to leave, an obviously hungover Angela finally appeared at our table. After a cup of coffee, she challenged us once again. "This is so dumb – let's just take a cab. We could get there so much faster, and they'll never know."

"No," I said, "we've voted. We have all agreed that after five weeks of training, one misstep could end our careers." I waved her to a seat.

TWA wanted us to learn the various ways to get to work in New York. Hangar 12 was the administration offices for both TWA pilots and hostesses, and it was also a repair facility for aircraft. A cab drive to get there was not allowed – our instructions, given to us the night before, were to take the subway to Queens, where we would then catch a local bus to Hangar 12.

"How was your night on the town?" Becky asked, trying to lighten the mood. "You look like death warmed over."

Angela reached for a cigarette. "I felt great until I came down here. Thanks for the compliment, Becky."

"You'll find no sympathy here," I said. "Are you going with us or not?"

She sighed. "Yes, I don't want you getting lost or mugged on the subway. It's only two blocks, but anything could happen."

We stepped out of the hotel and gradually worked our way into a rush of humanity. Steam rose from manhole covers that peppered the street and sidewalk. Young students dressed in uniforms chanted sing-song verses in an exotic language. Nearby, a tiny dog crouched over a minuscule patch of grass as its elderly owner, dressed in an outrageous outfit which somehow matched those on the dog, stood patiently waiting for a positive outcome. Harried people pushing past somehow managed to miss her and bump into me instead.

We managed to find the opening to the subway with long metal stairs that guided us into the concrete world of commuters. I had only ridden buses to football games as a teenager, and before arriving here, I had never heard of the New York subway, which was – and is – a way of life for the inhabitants of the city who are well-rehearsed in using its vast network of train lines.

"Get your tokens out!" Angela shouted as she worked her way towards the front of the crowd of passengers. Short glances at other travelers yielded few smiles, even less looks of curiosity; everyone was in a great rush to get on the subway before the doors closed. I felt like a student on a field trip.

As we waited for our train, Angela gave us a quick briefing: "The subway is going to be packed with commuters; you're going to feel like a sardine. Don't look into anyone's eyes and don't speak to anyone. If someone touches you in an inappropriate way, yell at them to stop. Otherwise, stay in a group. We'll be getting off at Kew Gardens, so if somehow you get away from the group, that's where we're headed. From there we're taking the JFK bus and we'll be getting off at JFK Hangar 12. Everyone got that?"

The train ride was exciting and loud – and did I mention smelly? Graffiti covered the outside and inside of the train. There were no open seats, but we managed to stand as a group for the short ride. Fortunately, no "inappropriate touching" occurred, but lewd stares and a few crude remarks did.

Once we got off the train, we made our way up the station stairs. "People are so hostile here," said Mandy.

"Living in New York is like living in a fishbowl: you learn to be unapproachable. That seems like hostility, but it isn't," Angela said.

On the street, our bus sat idling. I could see it was filled with airline employees, recognizable by the array of uniforms.

The subway ride had delivered us from the frenzied city of Manhattan to the bedroom community of Queens. The homes were quaint. Gated yards filled with flowers reminded us of home.

Becky turned to one of the uniformed women who had just boarded and asked, "Sorry, may I ask, do you rent? Or do you own your home? It's such a pretty neighborhood. What's the name of this community?"

It seemed impertinent, but Becky was impervious to embarrassment. Her small-town Kansas upbringing and sweet demeanor always managed to disarm everyone.

The woman, who now sat near us, smiled and said, "This is called Queens. Most homeowners either rent a room or their entire home to crew members. It's great for us – the rents are manageable, and you can't beat the commute time to JFK." A few of the other girls smiled in agreement.

Angela, ever the Debbie Downer, especially with a hangover, asked, "That sounds lovely – so what's the downside?"

"Well, you must sign a one-year lease, and they want first and last month's rent and a hefty cleaning deposit upfront. No-sub lease and no roommates unless they are approved. These landlords are tough cookies; they have lawyers on retainers."

"How long have you lived here?" I asked.

"Three years. I've established trust with my landlady, so she allows me to have 'guests' on occasion with no fuss from her."

"Guests?" Mandy whispered.

"Boyfriends."

"Oh." Mandy blushed.

As the bus entered the outskirts of the airport, the scene changed. Massive hangars replaced houses as runways could be seen in the distance as jets lined up, awaiting their turn to depart.

Ours was the first stop. As we left the bus, several ladies wished us good luck

The hangar was filled with new hires from earlier classes.

"Ladies, welcome to JFK. My name is Ms. Riccolli, and I am a supervisor here."

I recalled that she was the supervisor who had met us the night before. Everyone clapped as she continued: "I can see you are very excited to fly. Unfortunately, I have some bad news – due to the slowdown caused by the Air Traffic Controllers nationwide, TWA has implemented it first ever 'reduction of force.'"

She went on to explain that a reduction in force was a furlough – we would still be employed by TWA but wouldn't be able to work. Rather than having us stay in New York with no means of financial support, they were sending us back home until the controllers settled their union matters with the government. We were to go home and wait for a call – it could take days, weeks, or maybe months, but when it was over, we would still have a job at TWA.

As she called our names, she handed each trainee an airline ticket. Glancing at mine, I saw I was on a nonstop at 4:00 P.M. out of JFK to LAX.

We all sat there, stunned. Some of the girls giggled.

It was safe to say that I was shocked. I had watched several newscasts at the academy about a possible strike by the air controllers, but somehow, I hadn't realized it might affect TWA.

"I don't want to go home!" one girl cried.

Angela whispered, "Great! I'm calling my dad and getting on the first train to Connecticut. And we're taking a cab back to the hotel – my treat."

"Aren't you upset?" I asked.

"No, why should I be? We still have a job and now we can go visit our families, too."

Back at the hotel, trainees were stuffing their suitcases into cabs – it seemed as if they couldn't get out of New York fast enough.

I was seated in First Class on a Boeing 747, another moment that I will always recall. The plane was immense, and it had that new car smell, all shiny and clean. Despite the excitement, I felt a sense of dread at having to return home so soon, and it was another blow to my self-esteem. I hoped that God's plans for me were still in effect – I needed to know if there was a purpose in it.

After four hours, the 747 landed, and my aunt picked me up at the curb. I gave her the paper that Clint Eastwood so graciously signed, slightly wrinkled but intact.

"How was it? Was he nice?" she asked.

"Yes, Aunt Vie. He was exceptionally nice, and very handsome, too."

"I can't wait to show this to the girls at the Boeing plant! This is so exciting. Look, he put my name on it!"

Now you have to meet my aunt. She worked at the Boeing plant every weekday from 8:00 A.M. to 4:00 P.M, never complaining about spinning microscopic wires over condensers for hours at a time. It made me so happy to see her so excited over a piece of paper, even one that was signed by the dreamy Clint Eastwood.

Maybe this furlough did have a purpose. I'd have to wait and see.

Once I was home, I made a trip right back to the beach. I had missed the sights and sounds of my childhood. As my car crested a familiar hill overlooking Redondo Beach, I saw it: my old friend, the Pacific Ocean, which was enjoying a moment of calm as its foaming waves caressed the pristine white beaches. The sky was clear blue, and its rays caused the water to sparkle as if a million stars sat on a plate of smooth glass.

I was home.

On the third day back, I met with my former boss at the restaurant.

He was happy to reemploy me, but I asked if I could wait a week before I strapped on the old apron – I was holding onto hope that the air traffic controller slow down would subside, and we would be recalled to work.

True to its word, two weeks later TWA called my home and told me to return on the next flight to Kansas City – my ticket would be waiting at the desk at LAX airport.

I also learned that since they needed more international hostesses, they were waiving the language qualifications for the new hires. The slowdown had changed the direction of my career, and I felt like God had intervened in my life once again. It would have taken years for me to be able to learn a new language and pass the TWA Berlitz test so that I could fly International. Instead, all I needed was two more weeks of training to qualify before I could return to New York.

Angela stood waiting next to the familiar red and white TWA bus as some of my old classmates boarded, this time with a few more items from home.

Becky squealed when she saw us. "Isn't this great? We're flying International now!"

We all hugged as we chatted on the drive to Overland Park, Kansas.

It was good to get back to Breech. I was excited to see what new things we would learn in the short two weeks.

The classes were shorter this time. Memorization was the key to our success. The instructors were more congenial and seemed to be more understanding. I struggled with the conversion of international currencies. Our pursers oversaw the money on our planes, but TWA felt we should all be knowledgeable. "If you have a full flight with different countries being represented, it is imperative that you handle your transactions rather than put the load on your pursers and Flight Service Managers. We are a team." The two weeks passed quickly. Graduation was anticlimactic. We gathered our bags and prepared to return to New York.

We found ourselves walking down the same hallway at the Lexington Hotel. The ancient keys were still impossible to use. The beds were still lumpy.

I felt a twinge of homesickness for the academy. I had become accustomed to the surroundings, so warm and safe, and the redundancy of the day-to-day life there. I even missed the old guards who had made our business their business.

I hoped New York would grow on me. But for now, I would once again check underneath my bed.

CHAPTER ELEVEN

THE LYDEN

On our first day back, Becky jumped out of bed at 6:00 A.M. Not one to "sit on her laurels," as her mom would say, she was determined to find us a place to live. Having studied the list of apartments, she decided to try the Lyden, which was only blocks from our hotel.

The Lyden Apartments were well known on Lexington Avenue as a "stew zoo." It was mismanaged by 300-pound woman, dressed all in black – ironically, her name was Mrs. Black – who had a penchant for little white dogs and Cuban cigars. Her husband had died years earlier, leaving her the building in his will along with his two Westies, Fric and Frac.

He had planned to rent to well-heeled retirees, but death defeated him before he could instigate his plan. After his passing, the property – with its location and seductive six-month lease agreements – became popular with airline employees. It was the first property written on the TWA list for new hires.

As Becky approached the doorman, he warned her that Mrs. Black was not a very nice person and was known to scare away strangers, especially early in the morning.

Becky smiled. "Well, she's never met me."

The doorman waved her towards a room next to the elevator. As she reached for the knob, paint crumbled from the decrepit door. Speaking just above a whisper, she called out, "Anyone home?" Then she knocked, ever so lightly, not wanting to disturb the possibly sleeping ogre.

A gravelly voice shouted, "Go away, unless you're paying your overdue rent!"

Determined, Becky eased the door open and bravely walked into the darkened room. There Mrs. Black sat, in an overstuffed chair with her two little white dogs resting on the opposite chair arms. They growled softly.

Her head was wrapped in a colorful turban, which hid unwashed hair and obscured the small, beady eyes that scanned Becky closely as she entered. A strong body odor, mixed with cigar smoke, permeated the windowless room.

"Good morning, Mrs. Black." Becky edged her way towards the woman. "I hear you might have a vacancy."

"Are you asking for a room? Then just ask. You have a weirdo accent — where are you from?"

"Kansas, I'm from Kansas. You know – the Wizard of Oz, and Toto!"

Becky flashed her a smile, but Ms. Black wasn't responding. "Are you a stewardess?"

"No ma'am." (Well, technically she wasn't – TWA girls were called hostesses.)

"Well, take a seat. Let's talk."

Becky realized that her rough and tumble upbringing as an Air Force child would come in handy. With her family's many transfers, she had learned to easily engage with strangers, and she hoped her negotiating skills would allow her to at least see a room – and perhaps even secure a lease.

Smiling her dazzling, toothy grin, Becky reached for one of the cigars that sat on the well-worn coffee table in front of her. "Do you mind?" she asked.

Smiling back, Mrs. Black joined Becky for a smoke. Becky realized that the scary Mrs. Black was just a lonely old woman who, because of her weight and lifestyle, had become unapproachable.

After some cajoling, and the shared Cuban stogie, Mrs. Black revealed that she had just evicted five tenants who were employees of TWA. It seems they had tossed a rather large chair out of the window of their apartment at a group of construction workers, and that it had landed very close to a police officer standing on the ground below. This had caused quite a stir – the police officer was unharmed but demanded justice.

As Mrs. Black relived the story, the two little dogs hopped up on Becky's lap and licked her face affectionately.

"They like you," Mrs. Black said. "That's rare. I consider them my character cops; they help me decide on who I can rent to."

"Would you like me to walk them?" Becky asked.

Mrs. Black smiled and pointed to the leashes hanging on the door.

After Becky had completed the early morning stroll, Mrs. Black handed over a lease contract.

"I do work for TWA, as do my roommates," Becky confessed. "But I promise we won't cause any trouble, Mrs. Black."

"How many roommates?"

"There are five of us."

"Well, all I have is a one-bedroom apartment. It's small, but the other girls didn't seem to care. It's $1250 a month. And I will require a $500 down payment, right now."

"That's perfect." Becky smiled knowing she had won round one.

"Fill the contract out and get it back to me today. I'll reconsider based on Fric and Frac's decision." And then she laughed.

Becky, a Kansas girl accustomed to early mornings and unaccustomed to knocking, came bouncing into our room.

Jolted by Becky's buoyant footsteps, Angela rolled over, covering her head and moaning, "Get out, Becky. It's too early."

Angela was decidedly not a morning person – a cup of strong coffee and a cigarette were her morning friends. Ignoring Angela, Becky sat on the end of my bed recounting the morning's feat: "I found us a place!"

I sat up. "You did? Why, it's barely 7:00 A.M. It's dangerous to be out there alone." I was always the worrier.

"Oh, it was fine – not a bit scary. There are tons of people walking around – mostly drunk, but walking." She giggled. "But anyways, listen – we have a place and it's only four blocks from here. Isn't that great?"

"Yes, Becky that is just super. How much is the rent?" Angela asked from under her pillow.

"Well, cut to the chase, why don't you? Can I give you the details first?" Becky admonished.

Angela sat up. "That is a detail, dear."

"It's $1,250 per month."

Before Angela could respond, Becky expelled in one breath. "It's a one-bedroom, close to the bus station, around the corner from a bodega and right upstairs from a pizza place."

"What's a bodega?" I asked.

Angela groaned. "Stop trying to change the subject, Dianna. How are the four of us supposed to afford $300 a month in rent, when our monthly base pay is only $250? How about food? How do you suppose we pay for that?"

Becky shrugged. "Well, we can get another roommate along with Mandy."

"Mandy? Do you mean that goofy blonde who constantly complains about her weight, while she's stuffing her face?" Angela rolled her eyes. "She'll eat us out of house and home."

Becky laughed. "Hey, at least we know her faults. Better to know now than find out later. We only have to sign a six-month lease, so we can leave when we get off probation – it's perfect for us. All the places in Queens require a year lease, and I don't plan on staying here for a year. The landlady is crazy as a loon – I even had to walk her dogs – but we've got a lease."

"Walk her dogs...?" I asked. "Why on earth would you do that?'

"it's a long story, I'll tell you later" Becky sighed.

Angela reached for a cigarette. "Five girls in a studio – are you nuts?" She was surprised to find a cup of coffee waiting – Becky had thought of everything to entice approval out of Angela.

She gingerly offered Angela the Virginia Slims that sat near her bed. "Hey, if we all fly as much as they say we will, it'll be fine. Two people have the bed, two people have the fold-out couch, and I'll sleep on the floor. I have my old college sleeping bag."

"If we do this, we rotate. You're not sleeping on the floor every night," Angela replied.

Becky held out a piece of paper. "I have the lease right here. Angela, would you mind reading it? I'm going to find Mandy and Shelly and tell them the good news."

"Who's Shelley? I asked.

"She's our fifth roommate. She's from Iowa – super quiet and won't eat much." She laughed as she walked to the door.

Later, as we were leaving, Becky whispered to me, "I sure hope the lease is okay, since I already gave the landlady a $500 deposit and she assured me I wouldn't get it back if we changed our mind."

Angela overheard. "Becky, why would you do something stupid like that?" she demanded.

"I just know this is the right place! It's close to the bus station; it has a 24-hour doorman, a pizza shop next door that sells pop, and a nifty pay phone on the wall so we don't get in trouble with the telephone company. What else do we need?"

I shoved her out the door. In the hallway we found Shelly Beaumont, who stood quietly as Becky shared the good news. Standing nearby, Mandy fidgeted.

Shelly, taller than us, was very cool and collected most of the time. Little was known about her – at the academy, she usually stayed in her room, opting out of joining in the group study or dinner. She had shared with Becky that an affair with a married man in her small Nebraska hometown had caused her embarrassed parents to send her into the arms of TWA.

Mandy interrupted, hungry as usual: "I'm in. Now let's go eat."

Sitting at breakfast, I brought up the topic of the apartment. I thought it best to discuss the "elephant in the room."

"I want you all to keep an open mind about this apartment today. The rent is pretty steep," I said.

"How steep?" Shelly interrupted.

"It's going to be $250 per person a month," Becky answered. I thought Becky was smart that she didn't say $1,250 a month which was very hard to imagine, especially on an empty stomach.

"That sounds reasonable to me," Shelly said. She smiled.

After breakfast, we all agreed to go and see the apartment. If we all liked it, we would room together.

As we walked down Lexington Avenue, I noticed how the New Yorkers stared at us. Five women, strikingly attractive, were not unusual in New York.

I mentioned this to Angela, and she laughed. "They probably think we are professionals. Either professional models or professional hookers!"

On the outside, the building exhibited two large colonnades that expertly hid the overused, antiquated vestibule. An outdated, dust-covered Vogue magazine sat atop a lone side table next to a worn-out sofa. This building clearly wasn't up to Angela's standards – I watched as she walked around making silent observations.

Becky, now friends with the landlady, had managed to cajole a key to our new apartment.

The building consisted of 15 floors connected by an out-of-date elevator designed to carry only six skinny people at a time. After we all squeezed in, it labored its way up to our floor. Shelly groaned as the sounds increased with each floor. It also reeked of an odor I couldn't quite identify, and the carpet was stained and ripped in several places.

Our room was one of six other rooms located on either side of the hall. Becky worked the room key into the lock until the door sprang open. The entry seemed tiny, and the carpet was a 'lovely' faded avocado green, threadbare and dirty. A large picture window sat over a painfully over-used couch. The small bedroom had a lumpy double bed and one small nightstand, and the bathroom was crammed with a dirty tub and stained shower. The kitchen was the only salvation – since none of us cooked, we decided it would help with the much-needed storage. Plus, it already contained the most important items, a corkscrew and a can opener.

The apartment wasn't attractive, but it would serve our needs. A quick two blocks to the Carey bus station provided a way to commute to all three airports, and we all agreed that we could stand anything for six months.

After formally meeting the doorman and delivering the signed contract to the landlady, we returned to the hotel to prepare for our move. There we were met with the next problem.

"How are we going to move all this stuff to the apartment?" Shelly asked as she looked at the piles of boxes and suitcases.

The pile looked bigger than it really was. For training, each girl was allowed to bring one suitcase – a white Samsonite suitcase became part of the uniform. After returning from home, we each managed to accrue a box which contained more clothes and shoes. On the side of the street, fifteen items looked like a massive pile.

"It's only four blocks. We'll get a cab," I suggested.

"Four blocks aren't a long way, but a taxi will not drive four blocks with a load of boxes and suitcases!" Angela replied drearily.

"They will if you pay them the right amount of money," the hotel bellman said, eavesdropping on our conversation.

"How much is the right amount?" Angela asked, looking into her wallet. She handed him ten dollars, and with a whistle he summoned a yellow cab.

As the cab jerked to a stop in front of the hotel, we could tell it had seen better days. A few prominent dents and a broken windshield revealed its sordid history. The driver, a Sikh with a full beard, frowned as a quiet conversation with the bellman ensued. The driver shook his head as the bellman continued to negotiate.

Within a minute, the doorman, sure of his decision, smiled and said, "Thirty bucks, one trip, bags only. You walk."

"No way!" Becky whispered loudly. "How can we trust him not to steal all of our stuff?"

Angela held up her hand to be silent. "He's a Sikh," she said. "He is absolutely trustworthy but not impervious to a woman. You need to learn your ethnicities, girl!"

The bellman, obviously understanding the outburst, turned and walked back to the cab. Another quiet conversation ensued as the driver eyed us with a devious grin.

The bellman returned. "Okay, one of you can ride, but the rest will have to walk. Only one trip for thirty bucks – final offer. He wants the blonde."

Angela smiled at the driver and spoke directly at the bellman from the side of her mouth, "You know he's ripping us off and we can turn him in, right?"

The doorman smirked at her. "It's true. It's more expensive, but he's not a moving company, so why don't you call one?"

Angela smiled. "Okay, we'll do it."

We worked with the driver and managed to get most of the luggage in the cab trunk and onto the seats. In the end, we each had to carry a suitcase on the walk to our new place. Angela left with the overloaded cab, and we began our trek.

It was only 2:00 P.M., one day after graduation. As we navigated through the fast-paced pedestrians, no one seemed to notice us this time.

When we arrived at the Lyden, Angela was busy placing the baggage on a cart with the help of our new doorman. We loaded the elevator with as many bags as we could, taking several trips. The hot, airless elevator creaked and groaned on its way to our new home.

As we entered the apartment, the suffocating heat hit us again. I opened a window.

Shelly immediately went about making a list of cleaning solvents that would be necessary to make it clean and habitable. She was a clean freak, and she would have to be a magician, too.

Looking out of the two large picture windows, we faced a building currently under construction. The building was so close that the workmen were clearly visible, and as if on cue, a couple of them, straddling beams, waved at us and threw kisses reminiscent of chorus girls gone bad.

Becky reminded us of the TWA eviction with the chair throwing incident. It had marred our reputation with Mrs. Black. Our first rule was to keep the shades shut.

Five of us would live together for six months in an apartment with few places to hide. Flying was essential, if not for our rent money, definitely for our sanity.

"Okay, first things first," Angela announced. "We need to call crew scheduling and leave this number for contact. Who has a dime?"

Handing over a jar of dimes, Becky giggled. "I've been saving them."

The pay phone hung precariously on the wall. Paint, which was supposed to cover the scribbles from the former tenants, was still damp. Angela dialed JFK Crew scheduling and we stood around, listening and hoping for some good news.

After hanging up the phone, Angela repeated what the crew scheduler had told her: "Okay, it works like this. Everyone is on reserve. We don't go anywhere until we are released. We are released if our name isn't called or if we are on legal rest."

She walked to the couch. "We call in every afternoon after six o'clock. A recording will list twenty names. If your name is in the top ten, then you will need to be ready to fly. So, you sit by the phone, bag packed, and wait. If you don't fly that day, you have a good chance of going the next."

Angela went on to explain that after we flew, we would need to have "legal rest," which would be determined by the number of duty hours. Until we learned the formula, it would be a guessing game to calculate how long our legal rest time would be. She added that there are 100 reserves in New York, and that we could be assigned to domestic as well as International, though most likely it would be International.

"One hundred! My God, we will never get to fly," Shelly breathed from the back of the room. "I am going to have to turn tricks on Lexington Avenue to pay for food!"

Becky punched her in the shoulder. "Shelly, stop it!"

"The most important part is," Angela continued, "no one can be on the phone for more than three minutes. Crew scheduling will attempt to call twice, and if they get a busy signal twice, they will go onto the next girl. The scheduler, depending on how busy he is, might write you up. So, no long conversations."

Everyone looked at Becky. "What are you guys looking at me for?" she whined. "You know I only talk in the early A.M.!"

We spent the rest of the day organizing our clothes – the small entry closet would hold our uniforms and shoes. We found a Woolworth store nearby, and we purchased everything we would need to make the apartment habitable, dividing the cost between us. We packed our crew kits for flights and stored the rest of our personal items in boxes, neatly lined up in the kitchen. The bathroom was tiny, so we agreed to leave our toiletries in the chest of drawers.

When it was time for dinner, we practiced walking to the bus station.

The Carey Bus Station was very close to the Holland Tunnel, which made this location a plus for airline commuters. On a good day, all three airports were within 45 minutes or less from of our place. We each purchased a book of 30 round trip bus tickets for $10.00 – that would last us a month or more.

Later that night, tired but happy, we retreated to the local pizza parlor, bought a couple of beers, and toasted our future at TWA.

CHAPTER TWELVE

FIRST FLIGHT – MAY 30, 1970

We had been informed by our neighbors that, according to a *New York Times* article, crime was "exploding" in Times Square. The article reported that pickpockets ruled the day, while the pimps and prostitutes ruled the night, drug dealers occupied abandoned buildings, and rapists and muggers were making Central Park impossible to enjoy.

While we continued to be somewhat naïve about the crime taking place around us, we were ever-vigilant, crossing the street and dodging traffic to avoid any creepy-looking guys who might be following us.

Life wasn't idyllic – until we flew, our budgets, for example, were tight. In the meantime, we entertained ourselves with the many free museums and concerts that sprang up all over the city. Always traveling in pairs, we browsed through bookstores and art galleries, avoiding the expensive tourist traps like the Empire State Building and the Statue of Liberty. A departing neighbor gifted us with a T.V., which was temperamental at best. When it worked, Geraldo Rivera on *Eyewitness News*, with a beat towards the unusual lifestyles of New Yorkers, had become our favorite entertainment.

Our paychecks came on the 25th of each month and we paid our rent first, ever fearful of eviction by our mercurial landlady. We even took turns walking her dogs, and we visited her when she seemed lonely. Then whatever money was left we used for food.

And thanks to our Pan Am neighbors, however, we had discovered the infamous "Happy Hour."

"Whoever thought up Happy Hour was a genius," Angela would declare, as she finished reading the food section of a *New York Times* that she often pilfered from the neighbors' front door on Saturdays. Each day, we would plot our next Happy Hour destination. If all worked well, our arrival at the restaurant would coincide with the thirsty business-men who were kind enough to purchase us a drink, which would open the floodgates to free food. The only difficult part was unwinding their lusty tentacles as we attempted to leave.

I soon discovered that the reserve list was alphabetical, which explained why my roommates were flying and I wasn't. With so many ahead of me, it was a month before the schedulers got to my name. In the meantime, I watched jealously as my roommates departed on international flights, and when they returned, they would regale me with important information, which I memorized in preparation for my promised journey.

When the call did come, it was for a much-desired six-day double crossing. The trip represented half a month's worth of the required flight time, and enough expense pay to refill my nearly empty checking account.

I took my uniform out of the small coat closet. I had watched my roommates dress in uniform and now I would be able to join their ranks. I put it on and looked at myself in the mirror. I loved how the material clung to my narrow waist, and the skirt was a perfect length, just below the knees. TWA continued to dress us demurely, unlike some of our competitors. I had a choice of green, yellow, or red as a uniform choice, and I had picked green and yellow. My top was a deep yellow, the color of my old '56 Chevy.

As I walked to the bus stop, I couldn't help but notice the smiles from the people on the streets. I was proud to be wearing the uniform, and excited to be taking my first trip overseas.

After arriving at the hangar, I checked my mailbox, which was stuffed with advertisements and a few FAA updates. Then I met with the grooming supervisor. She approved of my makeup, uniform, and hair, so I was good to go.

After getting lost, I finally located the briefing room. The room was small and barely held the five crewmembers, including the purser. I was replacing a hostess with 25 years' experience, and I found out later she was the most junior one on the crew. I was met with cold stares, and I knew instinctively that they had little respect for my three-month seniority.

The purser introduced me, and I made a small prom queen wave. The briefing was short: the flight was full, and the cockpit crew would meet us on the plane. Work positions had been established before I arrived; I could tell this was an "everyday workday" for the crew. As I had hoped, I would be working in the coach cabin – my greatest fear was working a galley. The thought of working a galley and cooking for over 100 passengers kept me awake at night. I had served meals before as a waitress but managing that many meals in a small airplane galley seemed daunting.

I learned later that the coach aisle was always the last position to be bid on, and that it normally went to the younger hostesses by default. It seemed fair to me; we were young and fit, and the senior hostesses had earned their opportunity to escape the coach passengers. They had purchased their freedom with the millions of miles they had walked up and down the aisles over the years – it was our turn to develop varicose veins.

As we rode the bus to the terminal, I had a chance to talk with my partner, Ingrid. Her light blonde hair, tied in a perfect bun, sat neatly on her collar. Her blue eyes, accented by soft blue eye shadow, sparkled as she spoke:

"So, Dianna, is it? You must already know that I am German by my accent. Have you ever been to Germany? It's beautiful there. Especially the Black Forest, with its crystal streams of cool water and glorious tall trees. I played in these streams for hours as a small *kind*, er child. Sorry, I forget to speak in English sometimes."

I was startled by her sharing of personal information. I was a total stranger and I knew more about her, in that moment, than she knew about me. She seemed lonely.

"No, I haven't ever visited yet," I said. "But it sounds lovely. I can't wait."

After a long silence, I said, "May I ask you a question?" When she nodded, I asked, "Why is everyone on this crew so cold to me? Not one smile from anyone but you."

"They are – how do you say? – *vorsichtig*, wary of you. Not just you, everyone new. Maybe they'll warm up to you if you make it through today."

That scared me a little bit, but I figured she might be kidding. It was hard to tell.

She giggled. "So, you know, they rarely speak to me, either. They are like a clique. I am glad to have someone to speak with. So, is this your first actual flight?"

I nodded. "Yes, it is."

The bus arrived at the terminal, and we began our long walk to the departure gate. The terminal was an amazing work of art imagined by Eero Saarinen. This was my first time inside the building, and I was excited to know that this was my workplace. The building was mostly concrete, and yet it felt warm and inviting. The long red carpets that led to the gates were very lush and thick. Lovely as they were, they clung to my high heels, and I tried not to stumble.

Noting this, Ingrid looked down and said, "Don't worry – it takes some time to get used to this carpet."

We entered the plane together. It was my first time on a Boeing 707 and the cool air enveloped me as I looked down the long aisle filled with an endless line of passenger seats. How would I ever manage today? How many cups of coffee or tea would I spill?

Ingrid sensed my trepidation. "Come on, girl – let's go!"

After we reached the very rear of the plane, she sat her crew kit sideways on a seat. In a business-like tone, she said "There's so much to learn 'on the line.' Our academy trainers just can't pack everything into a curriculum. So, I'll try to fill in the blanks."

"What does 'on the line' mean?" I asked.

"It just means flying, you know, working. Just that. Okay, let's get to it." She pointed to the back of the last row of seats. "Stow your crew kit here but remember to get your serving smock and in-flight shoes out – you can't work a flight with those three-inch heels on." She laughed.

After instructing me to complete my emergency preflights and to locate my demo equipment, she continued with the instructions: "Commissary might open every cabin door the minute we arrive at the gate in Europe, so disarm your slide as soon as we park. Last week, they opened the first-class galley door that was still armed. An employee was knocked off the food truck, the flight was canceled – it was a mess."

I gasped. "Did he die?"

"Who?"

"The guy that fell."

"No, thank God, but he had some nasty injuries."

As we were talking, the captain appeared and requested a meeting in the First-Class cabin. He was very tall, with a leonine head. Silver hair spilled from his cap.

"Good morning, all. It's another full boat," he said. "Listen for our announcement, which might happen as we approach Newfoundland – turbulence has been reported, so you must keep the passengers seated until I turn off the seatbelt sign. Three knocks to enter the cockpit."

He turned to me. "We have a new hire on board today – Dianna, is it?"

"Yes, Captain. That would be me." This was my first encounter with a real airline captain. Just like every other girl I knew; I always found a man in a uniform handsome and mysterious. This tall, powerful man was no exception.

"Well, Dianna, welcome aboard. Have you ever flown on a 707?"

I shook my head. "No, sir."

Ingrid said, "Captain, this is her very first flight! Isn't that exciting?"

"That's great. When you get a chance, come and see us. We haven't laid eyes on a new hire for a very long time, so this is quite refreshing." He shook my hand.

"Thank you, sir." I could feel a rosy heat all over my face. I also felt a very intense stare coming from one of the women, whose name I couldn't recall.

I returned to the galley with Ingrid, anxious to continue my lessons. When we got back there, Ingrid immediately admonished me.

"Stay away from the captain," she warned. "Helen in First Class has her claws in him." *Helen, yes – that was her name.*

I wanted to ask how I was supposed to stay away if he wanted me to visit the cockpit? It was a small airplane, after all. But I decided to work on that later.

She handed me a menu. "Hand out menus as you sell headsets. After we get in the air, we will get the liquor cart ready. Sell the wine! That will not only help keep the meal service moving, but it will also keep your trays easier to carry – wine splits are heavy."

I nodded. "That makes sense."

"By the way, the movie is 'Love Story' with Ryan O'Neal and Ali McGraw. Remember that the movie is free, but the headsets cost $2.50." She laughed. I had heard this is in training – TWA could ill afford the thousands charged for each movie reel, so they decided to charge the passengers.

"Don't plan on sitting and watching the movie; we'll be serving drinks the entire flight. Keep an eye on the smokers – no standing and smoking. And especially keep an eye on the ones who will try and take their cigarettes into the lavatory. A fire in a lavatory won't do."

Ingrid walked over to the galley and began opening drawers. I could not imagine storing and serving enough food for two meals in this small galley.

She turned and asked me "Are you listening?"

"Yes, I wish I could take notes."

"Trust me, you'll get this in no time. When we begin the food service, things will become extremely hectic. I will move fast and so should you. You need to know right away that I am very territorial when it comes to the galley – most galley hostesses are."

She drew an imaginary line with her foot. "Please never stand close behind me or come across this line. If I swing around with a loaded tray, the food might end up on you and most definitely on the floor."

It was refreshing to hear her instructions. To be honest, I was over-whelmed – I hoped I would recall all of this. At least I knew what she expected of me.

"If you need something," she said, "ask in one syllable, if possible: milk, cream, sugar."

She instructed me to collect ten small drink cups from the water foun-tain. "These will be our tea setups – always prepare these in advance. The Brits drink tea and the Americans drink coffee."

She began to demonstrate how to set up each cup – a sugar packet in the middle, one tea bag beside it, and a lemon slice on the other side. Five with lemon and another five with creamer for the Brits. "Never let the lemon touch the tea bag" she said.

As I was completing the task, she spoke again: "There are always three choices of meals: chicken, veal, and beef. That's all I want to hear from you when you return from the cabin – not chicken chasseur or beef Bourguignon. We change our menus about once every six months, so don't get too attached to the names of the entrées.

Our food is cooked on very hot, porcelain plates. Use these hot pads if you must touch them. Also, remember to remove the foil. I avoid touching them with my fingers if I can help it. Are you getting this?"

"Yes, you're a very good instructor."

She smiled. "Now, Europeans are always curious about the ingredients of their food. When they start asking, just say, 'We have some of the finest chefs in America, and I'm not one of them.' They will hopefully laugh."

"Have you ever been a waitress?"

I nodded. "Yes."

"Did you enjoy your job?" I nodded again. "Good, that will really come in handy. One more thing – whatever you do, don't get into any long conversations. This dinner service can take hours if we don't keep it rolling. If I think you've been out there too long, I'll run out the next order and give you an ugly look – it will remind you to stop socializing."

As we continued our preparations, there were more detailed instructions from Ingrid: "Do not overload drinks with ice – two cubes should do it for the Americans. More than that and we will run out. Ask if they want ice – Europeans prefer their drinks without. And also, no full cans of mixer unless it's a double."

I nodded my head again. I had heard all of this in training, but I was relieved to be reminded.

"The purser will help with our liquor service as soon as he's finished with his liquor service in First Class. We serve from the back to the front, and he'll serve drinks to the first four rows and then meet us on the cart. He will also pour coffee during our dinner service. All you'll need to do is run trays out."

As I stood mulling over the menus, the purser appeared.

"So, ladies," he said, "are we ready?" Before we could answer, he addressed me directly: "Has Ingrid filled you in on the meal service? She's a very professional galley hostess; you are lucky to fly with her. She will have you running your cute little bum off, but you will be a pro at the end of this six-day marathon. Do you have any questions for me?"

I smiled. "No, no questions."

"Alright then, we will begin boarding the passengers. Dianna, I want you in the aisle. Please make sure no one puts anything other than a coat or a hat in the overhead compartment. If we get the turbulence that the captain is predicting, everything will be on the floor. By the way, when that is happening, do not get up from your jump seat until you hear four bells."

Before long, passengers began filling the First-Class cabin. A handful of languages could be heard as everyone nestled themselves in the larger, wider seats.

Next, the coach passengers spilled into the cabin. I carefully guided a few suitcases from the overhead to the floor, and I could hear the purser speaking over the P.A., stressing the need to use the cabin floor for bags. He spoke in several different languages, including English.

Selling the headsets was a challenge. Language wasn't a barrier, but currency exchange was – most of the customers carried U.S. currency, but some wanted to try out their newly purchased British pounds and German deutsche marks. The purser stayed near me and made the exchanges with ease, explaining later that the airlines had an excellent exchange rate that passengers loved to use. I made a mental note to "bone up" on my rates of exchange when I got to my layover room.

After nearly an hour, with the passengers all settled in, we began our roll down the long runway at JFK. The plane slowly lifted, and I felt my pulse quicken. I was ready to join the international party. This was it: the long preparation and training would now be tested.

The liquor service was a breeze, with Ingrid translating the choices, and I sold wine and an occasional headset. When the purser arrived to relieve Ingrid, she proceeded to the galley, and I soon followed her.

Serving the meals was very frustrating, as no one appeared to have even glanced at the menus. It seemed I was continually giving a detailed explanation regarding the choices of entrees, ingredients, and accoutrements. I learned quickly to walk a few rows ahead each time and "warn" the customers that I was coming to take their dinner orders, hoping they would get the hint.

Ingrid was pleasant and professional, never losing her cool with me as I wiggled and stumbled down the aisles, trying to juggle the trays and dodge arms and feet. I could barely see over the food – anyone who questions the abilities of a hostess carrying two loaded trays with heavy porcelain dishes and wine splits down an aisle during turbulence without spilling anything needs to try it, just once.

Halfway through the service, bells chimed through the cabin as the First Officer spoke to the passengers: "We are entering an area of reported turbulence. Please return to your seats immediately and fasten your seat belt. Hold onto your drinks. We should be through this in around five minutes."

The five minutes was more like 20 minutes, and Ingrid used the time to reload her ovens with fresh, uncooked meals, while I sat snugly buckled in the jumpseat, wondering if she was going to get in trouble with the seatbelt gods if she didn't sit down. There were so many supervisors at the academy, and I just knew there had to be one on this jet.

I could hear the passengers oohing and awing over every dip, and I was hoping I wouldn't have a mess to clean up when the turbulence was over. I was reminded of our "Fright Flights" at the academy – this turbulence was fun, plus I enjoyed the chance to rest.

When Ingrid finally sat down, she explained that there was turbulence for passengers and turbulence for hostesses. This turbulence, a milder form, was the kind that only hostesses could move around in. "Best to stay in the back though. If they see you up, they totally disregard the seat belt sign."

I knew that I would eventually figure this out, but for the time being, I decided to follow the cockpit's requests.

The most difficult part of the flight was picking up the empty trays. I picked some up as I was returning to the galley for my next orders, and soon discovered that I had made a huge mistake. In doing so I had loosened a score of passengers from their captive tray tables, and they began milling about the cabin or standing in line for the bathroom, making it nearly impossible for me to make my way to the first rows.

Ingrid smiled at me when I commented on this, assuring me that with time I would learn to leave the passengers confined to their seats until I was finished serving everyone; it was an art that took time to cultivate.

"Passengers are like cattle," she said. "The minute they chew their cud, they've got to take a shit." It sounded pretty funny with her German accent.

Laughing at her own joke, she reached out to pat me on the back. "You've done well for a first-timer. It will become easier."

"Thank you, I think."

The movie began after we had sold duty free liquor to the Americans, who were positive that they couldn't afford to buy scotch in England. The movie did not keep the smokers and drinkers entertained, though, and they insisted on continuing the party in the back by the galley. Smoke layered itself over the entire airplane, engulfing the few breaths of recycled air. The smokers stood, despite being continuously "cautioned" about not smoking while standing or using the lavatories."

The aroma from the overused lavatory, mixed with the exotic European cigarette smoke, became overwhelming. Ingrid assured me that I would eventually get used to it. *Not likely*, I thought.

My trip to the cockpit was brief, fearing retribution from Helen. I was in awe of the pilots – not only were they managing to fly, but they had memorized the thousands of buttons and knobs that jutted all around me. I had decided that they must be very smart, indeed.

Fighting sleep was a continuous battle. I stayed on my feet, ignoring the lure of the comfy-looking jumpseat, always moving to stay awake. When the sun peeped through the few open window shades, my eyes screamed as if sand had been sprinkled on them; they begged to be closed.

It seemed like an eternity until the captain spoke over the P.A., announcing the Irish coastline. We had served a quick continental breakfast service that included orange juice, a sweet roll, and coffee. The smoker and drinkers who had partied at my expense were sound asleep, and interrupting their slumber for our arrival was my sweet vengeance.

We handed out the customs forms to the passengers deplaning in England, while the captain announced the weather in London.

When we landed, I smiled – our Big Boeing 707 had delivered us safely. Through the haze of exhaustion, I felt a surge of excitement returning. I was in London – even if I was stuck on the plane and unable to visit Big Ben, I was still in England!

Ingrid shook my hand. *"Glückwunsch*! Er – congratulations," she said. "You are now an international hostess."

CHAPTER THIRTEEN

EVACUATION: JUNE 24, 1970

TWA began flying the 747 in February 1970. As with all the newer airplanes, there were many yet-undiscovered idiosyncrasies, and each new discovery on the 747 was addressed with company memos. These would in turn be followed by FAA directives. We often found ourselves operating in a minefield of safety and service.

As I boarded my plane in Madrid for a return to New York, I breathed in that "new car" smell that permeated the cabin – the aircraft was pristine, with rows and rows of blue seats accented with a bright red stripe. TWA spared no money when it came to its brand; our seats, designed with individually-controlled lumbar support, demonstrated how devoted we were to passenger comfort. No other airline paid for this expensive addition.

The senior, more experienced hostesses, opted to bid the Boeing 707, instead of the brand-new 747, and they would watch from afar as we, the junior ones, worked out the kinks. Most, if not all, of us juniors had just graduated from the academy; on this day, at the age of twenty, I was the second-to-last on the seniority list.

The briefing that morning was long and noteworthy, and I felt nervous. I listened intently, knowing I had a lot to learn. After the Service Manager completed the bidding process for work positions – because we all had just graduated, we bid our positions by age – the director of customer service immediately began to speak. He pointed out our customers had been having trouble opening the newly-designed overhead bins – the shorter passengers couldn't access the handles, while others just couldn't figure out how to use them.

It was understandable, I thought. The 747 was the first airplane to offer overhead storage bins for baggage; prior to this, passengers were required to store all luggage underneath their seats. Only coats and hats were allowed in the overhead bins.

"You are now tasked with opening the overhead bins right after landing," the DCS said. "You are to walk through the cabin right after thrust reversal, open all the bins in your zone, and then quickly return to your assigned doors before arriving at the gate. Do not hand out items. And be quick about it." When you consider that the landing speed of a 747 was around 160-175 MPH, this policy probably seemed incredulous. However, at the time service was "king," and until after the incident that was about to occur, it trumped safety.

Our load this day was full – it seemed everyone wanted to experience the 747. I ended up at the R5 door. There are ten doors on the 747, five on the left and five on the right, and I was on the right-hand side, at the last door closest to the tail.

My passengers were all Spanish-speaking, with a sprinkling of translators, and I also had a large group of Spanish professors traveling to Columbia University for a conference. During my safety demonstration, I made a point of illustrating how easy it was to open and close the overhead storage bins – I figured my passengers were intellectual enough to use this information later.

Halfway through our flight, the movie broke. The large film canister lay on the center seats as the Flight Service Manager managed to splice and rewind the spool, while the inconvenienced passengers were entertained with free cocktails. Once the film was restarted, everyone was seated, and the rest of the trip proved to be uneventful.

With custom forms handed out and cabin checks completed, I took my jumpseat for landing. The 747 descended slowly over Long Island, and my eyes fought to stay open. It would be so easy just to close them and fall into that world of serene calm sleep that I so craved – and the gentle swaying of the airplane wasn't helping any.

The engines subtly changed pitch, which signaled that our flaps would soon be extended – landing was not far off. Though the concave design of the small door windows made everything appear fuzzy, I could just begin to see the outline of land.

As we approached JFK, my passengers began to chatter amongst themselves. I felt the unmistakable touch of our wheels on the pavement as the giant engines reversed to slow our forward momentum. The landing was perfect, and the passengers began to clap. The Service Manager announced, "Ladies and Gentlemen, welcome to New York!"

As I unbelted my seatbelt to begin my walk through the cabin, I noticed a thin layer of white smoke resting near the floor of the cabin. What was leftover from the European cigarettes was finally beginning to clear, as the reusable cabin air was being automatically refreshed from the outside. I hated the God-awful cigarettes – my bloodshot eyes burned from both a lack of hydration and eight hours of enduring cigarette smoke.

I quickly made my way through the cabin, opening the bins. I would occasionally hand out an item, even though we had been instructed not to – it was easier to hand things out, than argue in a language in which I wasn't conversant.

The plane was still moving quickly down the runway. But as I finally reached the R4 door, it had slowed precipitously. I then turned around to make my way back to my door. Suddenly, however, I heard the unmistakable high pitch of the evacuation alarm. (That all-too-familiar sound reverberated through my head, even in my sleep, from the daily dose I had received at the academy.)

As I looked down at the R4 jumpseat, the continuous flashing of the red evacuation light unquestionably reminded me that we needed to get off the airplane – and fast.

Even though I was standing at the R4 door, it wasn't *my* exit door, and I knew I had to get back to my passengers. I began working my way through the cabin as fast as possible, considering all the passengers were now up and totally unaware of the danger.

As I pushed past them, they grabbed me to ask questions, but I ignored them, elbowing the old ladies who attempted to stop me – I had to get to my door. I stretched my neck to see if I could see my partner on the other side of the cabin.

Soon, an announcement was made: "Ladies, this is an evacuation. Proceed to your doors!"

Easy for you to say, whoever you are, I thought. A memory of my instructor saying that we had exactly ninety seconds to get everyone off the plane haunted me as I worked my way to my door.

Realizing that I would not be able to push my way through the throng of passengers, I began climbing over the tops of the seats. This was a task, considering that my checkerboard skirt was not as short as it needed to be. Even so, I managed to work my way slowly to the rear of the cabin, pushing away clinging passengers until I finally found my door.

As I rotated the handle of the over-300-pound door to free the evacuation slide from its housing, adrenaline shot through my veins. A "whoosh" sound was accompanied by a strange, sweet smell that stung my nose as I gulped for air. The door easily and automatically swung open, and the slide fell to earth in a voluminous explosion of gray. The outside world became silent.

I realized I needed to take the next step, to see if my slide was safely and fully inflated. My training kicked in; I reached for the door handles to thrust my body over the door and inspect the slide's performance. Considering that the door sat nearly ten feet above the ground, an under-inflated slide would mean certain death for my unsuspecting passengers.

Sirens from airport fire trucks joined the internal cacophony of the cabin – the passengers had finally realized that we were attempting to get them to safety, away from an unrecognized threat.

Shouts from the firemen outside my door, combined with them throwing hand signals at one another, caught my attention, and I watched my slide land near a newly parked fire truck.

Small wisps of white smoke from the number four engine began to drift in the direction of my door, and it was then that I became terrified – were we on *fire*?

The shouts of the firemen became clearer – they were telling me to go to the other side of the plane. The problem was on my side, and it would be too dangerous to send the passengers that way.

As I turned, a pair of hands suddenly encircled my waist. Moments later, I found myself upside down in the small coat compartment located behind my door, my head throbbing.

I cannot recall my actions after I hit my head on the wall of the coat compartment. The doctors later said that the concussion I received wiped my memory.

A "mysterious man" had pushed his way from the other side of the plane, accidentally knocking out my partner, perhaps with his elbow. We think he imagined he was rescuing me falling out of the plane. According to passengers, I climbed out of the coat compartment with what a passenger would later describe in the FAA Report as 'fire in my eyes'.

As I said, I remember very little of what happened next, though it seems I may have endured some additional combat with the mysterious man before he was evacuated along with all the passengers in the E zone, the last zone in the aircraft. I learned later that he was a newly-returned Vietnam vet, who was experiencing "positive panic."

We were taught during training that there were two types of panic, Negative panic was when a passenger becomes immobile due to fear. I remember my instructor saying that we might have to scream or slap the individual to get them to move. *Then there's positive panic*, the instructor had said. *This is the dangerous kind.* A passenger, such as the man I encountered, realizes the danger and starts to take control of the situation. It is imperative that we be in command to ensure the safety of our passengers.

After the evacuation was all over, rescuing firemen found me sitting in a cabin seat. I had suffered a concussion, a bruised rib, and a fractured arm. My partner on the other side was injured as well – my attacker's elbow had broken bones in her face.

It was later discovered that the engine was not on fire, but that someone had seen smoke coming out of the number four engine as we landed and flipped the evacuation alarm. "Where there's smoke, there's fire" was not the case this time.

The communications between the cockpit and the cabin crew tightened up after this first TWA evacuation of a 747. Also, the company policy of hostesses opening the overhead bins and handing out passengers' belongings after thrust reversal was discontinued.

It took much longer for the FAA to change the seatbelt policy, but eventually passengers were reminded to stay in their seats until the seat belt sign was turned off. "Barber poles" were also added to the slides. These inflatable poles would pop up along the length of the slide, eliminating the need to thrust oneself over the door to check the proper slide inflation.

The reported occurrence of smoke was never fully explained to us, and I'm not confident there was a plausible explanation – it is just one of those unexplained idiosyncrasies. To my knowledge, it never happened again on another flight.

CHAPTER FOURTEEN

WINE....ANYONE?

TWA Hangar 12 sits just on the perimeter of the runway at JFK Airport. Everyone based at JFK, whether a hostess or pilot, would eventually call this place home. Its long narrow hallway has myriad rooms that serve as the administrative offices, mail rooms, and crew briefing areas.

Today, I was doing my best to hide from my supervisor, who I knew was looking for me. My mailbox held several requests to come to her office, and they had started to take on a somewhat ominous tone. Incident reports were rare, but when an "incident" occurred, supervisors interviewed everyone who had worked on the flight, and then used that information to respond to the customer. Even though we were in the jet age, customer comments were filtered down via Pony Express.

Hostesses had to defend any questionable comments, even though they rarely had a memory of the passenger or incident. I remembered a senior telling me on my first flight that the bad letters don't get to you for around three months – three months is a long time to remember details when you are sitting on the hot seat in front of a supervisor being asked a load of questions. I had become diligent about using the flight log provided by the company. It helped jog my memory, especially in moments like this.

She found me.

"Hey, girl," she said, "I've been looking for you."

Mrs. Bernadette Shapiro, who preferred to be called Bea, was an aristocratic-looking woman. She stood around 5'7", including her stylish Angela Davis afro, and she commanded and received respect from hostesses and pilots alike. As one of the first black women to be hired by TWA, she had worked tirelessly to secure the title of supervisor. She was direct and affable, with a contagious belly laugh. She spoke three languages with a smattering of Hebrew. She was instrumental in redesigning the meal service for the flights to Tel Aviv.

"I heard," I said. "I'm sorry, I've been flying. I keep missing you when I'm here." *On purpose,* I thought.

"This won't take long. I just need a statement regarding a flight you took last month."

As we entered the anteroom, several other supervisors smiled. I had only been here once before, when I first arrived in New York City. That occasion was so different – I was a fresh recruit then, bathed for a short time in the love that only a new hire feels. On this occasion, however, I felt like an animal that had been hunted down for information.

"I'm just a little uncomfortable," I said.

"You have nothing to fear; you are not here because you have done anything wrong. We just need to get a few more details. Every other member of the cabin crew has already been interviewed, and you are the last piece of the puzzle."

I squirmed under her gaze. "I was hoping that you would overlook me since I am so junior," I said shyly.

"So, you already thought you'd be coming in to see me about this?"

"Well, you just never know. Everyone's impression of your actions is different."

She looked at me with a wry smile. "Ms. Dianna, I repeat: you are not in trouble. Now I want to know what you recall about a domestic flight you took about two months ago. It was a flight from St. Louis to Las Vegas, an inaugural service – 'Wines of the World,' I think it was called. We received several commendation letters."

A wave of relief swept over me. Orchid letters – yes! Good letters, not bad ones. I should have been excited about the commendation letters – I was still on probation and any good letter couldn't hurt. But something was eating at me about this flight, and I couldn't grasp what it was.

I searched my memory. I stared at the desk quietly, my hands perspiring, until I remembered my logbook.

"I'll try," I said. "May I look at my trip log so I can refresh my memory?"

"Excellent, I was hoping you had one. Lots of hostesses think they are nonsense, until moments like this. Go ahead." She pointed to my purse.

"I have only worked one domestic flight," I said, as I thumbed through the log. As I found the page, I read the following words, written in my own writing: *Peggy and Panty Hose*. I knew instantly that trouble could be brewing here.

It began so innocently, this flight with the Infamous Peggy Iwanowski.

I was on reserve, so I could be assigned to both domestic and international flights. When the phone rang, I was excited about flying to Europe.

"Las Vegas?" I asked. "Are you sure? I'm supposed to fly international."

"You're supposed to fly wherever I tell you to." The grumpy crew scheduler sounded angry. "I don't like sending you to Las Vegas any more than you do – it's some new service and they need a someone who can open wine."

Even more confused, I looked up the flight. It left out of La Guardia – it would be my first time back there since I first arrived in New York. The flight would make a stop in St. Louis and then proceed on to Las Vegas, where I would lay over and fly back the next day on the same route.

My roommates were of no help – they said they had heard that with no supervision, domestic hostesses were laid back and irresponsible. International crews had Directors of Customer Service (DCSs), Service Managers, and Pursers to guide them along. Domestic crews just had each other.

I learned that TWA was inaugurating a new wine service for the St. Louis to Las Vegas flights – our flight would be the first flight to do so. We would be serving upscale, full-sized bottles of wine, enhanced by a newly designed food service.

Wine had been served on these flights before, but they were a cheaper California brand in splits, with screw tops. Passengers who were transferred from international flights had lodged complaints about the inferior wine choices, and they had won their case for a better quality of wine.

I personally think the change had more to do with the fact that Braniff Airlines was now serving a higher quality of vintage wines, thus eating away at our market share.

When the call came from the scheduler earlier that day, he had confided that they needed someone from International who could open wine. That may sound a little lame, but trust me, opening a bottle of wine on an airplane is a bit more complicated than it may seem.

Pressurization causes wine to stay neatly corked away. Dry corks are also an ongoing problem, especially when the bottles are not properly stored. This would be the first time that domestic commissaries would deal with large, corked bottles of wine.

So, I knew how to open a bottle of wine – but what I didn't know at the time was that I was flying with a hostess known for her on-board antics; she was written up more times than any other. The ironic part was the number of her good letters outnumbered her bad letters. With that and the protection of the union, she continued to fly unabated. The stories about her were legendary.

When I arrived at the airport, I immediately became lost – I was clueless as to the location of Operations.

As I wandered around looking for a sign of some type, I heard a melodious voice with a thick Southern accent. It was coming from the hostess walking far ahead of me – she was shouting at the gate agents as she passed their respective gates, who then waved and smiled as she blew kisses to each of them.

I quickened my pace in order to catch up with her. Considering she was carrying her crew bag in addition to a rather large box, she was amazingly fast. The next thing I knew, I was following her downstairs.

The stairs led to a hallway, which led to several doors. Setting the box on the floor, she swung open the door to the Operations office. I heard someone yell, "Peggy!"

Two other hostesses stood at the Operations desk, one signing a paper on a clipboard.

Peggy stopped abruptly, and I ran right into the back of her. She turned. "Hi," she said, "are you going to Las Vegas?"

"Yes, I am," I said. "Sorry, I didn't mean to run over you."

"I stopped too quickly. I drive worse, which is why I don't drive. I'm Peggy Iwanowski – and you are?" She held out her hand.

"I'm Dianna Shockley."

"Well, welcome to our little Las Vegas run. You're new, aren't you? You're the international hostess – I can tell."

"You can? How?"

Before I discovered her secret, she followed up with, "Have you ever flown a 727 before?"

"No, this is my first domestic flight." I was pleased that she already knew I was fresh out of the academy. It was a relief not to have to announce it to the crew every time I came to work.

One of the two hostesses walked over and gave Peggy a hug. "Hey, chief," she said. "How's my favorite hell-raiser?"

"I'm great. Are you girls ready for a weekend of fun and frolic in 'Lost Wages'? I have tickets for Wayne Newton and The Supremes." Peggy beamed.

"Wonderful. Think we'll have time to gamble?" The hostess looked over at me. "Last week Peggy won over $500 at the blackjack table."

I wasn't sure if this exchange was for my benefit or if all domestic crews were this informal and fun-loving. I was rather enjoying the camaraderie that this crew seemed to have – international crews were somewhat subdued and less extroverted.

"Dianna is an international hostess who was assigned to help us with the new service that we are inaugurating today," Peggy said with a smile. "In case you didn't get to your mailboxes yet this week."

"I've never flown a domestic flight," I said. "I'm a little nervous."

Peggy shook her head. "Oh, don't worry – we're pretty easy-going around here. We may not be as snotty as the international babes, but we're better looking – right, girls?"

The other two girls smiled a coy smile. I noticed Peggy had an interesting face, which became sexier by degrees when she smiled. Her thick Southern drawl accentuated the facial expressions that she obviously had practiced with a purpose. Her straight brown hair surrounded a round, pixie-like face, and dark brown eyes that flashed with a devilish twinkle. Around 5'7", her buxom figure was impressive.

"Dianna – is that what you want us to call you?" Peggy asked. I nodded.

"Well, my name is Pawla, but you can call me Peggy. This is Lorraine and Alice. I am senior on this trip, so we'll dispense with the formalities. Lorraine and Alice will work coach and you and I will work first class. I will be working in the cabin, and you will work in the galley. Have you ever worked in a galley? Other than training, I mean?"

"Yes, I worked a 707 to Greece last month." I replied, starting to feel my anxiety rise at the thought of working in a domestic galley.

"Well, the first-class galley on a domestic flight is a hell of a lot easier than an international flight. The only difference is time – international flights have time and domestic have none. I'll see you all at gate 50 in ten minutes. I've got to go and drop this box off at the ramp. It's a baby gift for Sam.

The other two girls followed Peggy, and I signed myself in. I looked around at the office – it was much smaller than the vast operations complex at JFK. I took a moment to explore the crew room down the hall, which did not impress me either. It was filled with several lounge chairs and old copies of *Vogue* magazines. Three women dressed in colorful, paisley lounging pajamas lay haphazardly across the couches. I was impressed that they had managed to wear their pajamas in the crew lounge. I wanted to compliment them on how pretty they were, but they were asleep.

I left for the gate, not wanting to get lost again. After a few minutes, I saw my crew. They were all laughing and talking. When I caught up to them, I mentioned the women in the crew lounge.

"Pajamas? You didn't say that to them, did you?" Peggy asked.

"No, I would have, but they were asleep."

They began to laugh hysterically. Peggy snorted, which caused the other two women to laugh harder.

I waited to see what was so funny. Peggy, coming up for air, said, "Pajamas!" and it started all over again.

Finally, they calmed down enough to say that those girls flew for Braniff, and the "pajamas" are their uniforms, designed by Pucci. "They are pretty touchy about them," Peggy said. "I mean, wouldn't you be?"

She waved at the gate agent. "Okay, we can board in ten minutes."

After stowing our belongings and doing our cabin preflights, we stood quietly, listening as Peggy read a from a memo regarding the new service.

"We have to make sure our oven counts are correct before leaving," she said. "New York Commissary is boarding the food."

The girls groaned, and I looked at them quizzically. "LaGuardia Commissary is famous for messing up the galley provisioning," one girl said. "They always short us on coach meals. So, then we end up making do. You rob Peter to pay Paul – like stealing first class leftovers to make a coach meal. It's not fun."

I was surprised; that was not something that we dealt with on international flights. Our DCS's oversaw the food counts long before they made it onto the airplane.

"The wine will be boarded in St. Louis," Peggy continued. "God help us if they don't do it right. With galley supplies like tea, coffee, and that stuff, I want to know, now, not later."

She turned. "Lorraine, you know how slow Commissary is here. If you're short on anything, call me and I'll get on the horn to Sam downstairs." Lorraine nodded and left, walking back to the galley at the rear of the Boeing 727.

"We are full in first class and coach all the way to Vegas. I think the General is coming on board for a briefing, so come back up here after you've finished counting."

The other hostess then walked back to join Lorraine, and I stood in the 727 galley, trying to familiarize myself.

"So, you ready for this, girlie?" Peggy stretched as she spoke. Her eyes were streaked with red, and she looked as if sleep had not graced her the night before.

"I'm not really sure what I'm supposed to be looking for," I said.

She handed me a galley checklist. "I keep this on hand just in case. These are the 'must go' items – just start opening drawers and see what you find. By the way, the contents of a drawer are always listed on the front by Commissary. They started doing that in the last couple of months to help you new hires out."

As I started working my way through the galley containers, she asked how I liked the job so far.

"So far so good," I said. "But I'll let you know tomorrow. We only fly one trip every two weeks, and I was just getting used to flying international."

"Yes, domestic is really different," she said. "No pursers or flight service managers to do all the paperwork and decision-making. How do you like those new DCSs?"

I shrugged. "They're okay, I guess. Everyone seems to have a different opinion of them." I knew full well of the upheaval that the word Director of Customer Service had caused in the ranks of hostesses at TWA – a DCS represented management, and hostesses were very union, not wanting any kind of management on-board their planes at any time. The only acceptable form of management was the captain, who was also union.

The DCS had been added with the introduction of the Boeing 747. It made good sense. The new plane's inherent problems caused cancellations, and there was a need for immediate customer service that could not wait for landing. Their duties also included managing the cabin crew – that is where the line was drawn, and the trouble started.

"Well, let's check this galley out and see what's missing. When I finish with you, you'll know everything there is to know about a 727 galley."

We opened every door and drawer, finding sugar, creamers, extra butters and extra everything. Some of the metal carriers held clean porcelain dishes with no food – she explained that these were being sent to St. Louis for replenishing purposes.

After we finished looking through the galley, I must have looked like a deer in the headlights. "I sure hope I don't mess you up today," I said.

"Ah, darlin', don't worry. I'll take care of you." She touched my shoulder with an easy grace, and I felt she meant it.

"This flight is easy," she continued. "A short hop to St. Louis, then on to a night of sex and sin in Las Vegas! I'll have you trained in no time – you just watch my moves."

Peggy brushed her hands over her ample breasts and adjusted her uniform. Straightening her back and thrusting out her chest, she smiled a shit-eating smile that would have seduced a monk. I was naïve, but not that naïve – there was no question, this girl had moves. There was a simmering sensuality underneath that sweet, southern smile.

"I'll bird dog the wine, you guys just concentrate on the food." As she said this, a woman, obviously a supervisor, walked through the door of the 727.

"Damn – the General is here," Peggy said out of the side of her mouth. She smiled as she turned to address a tall, thin woman holding a clipboard in her hand. "Good afternoon, Adele."

The woman was a La Guardia Airport supervisor, who was, as I would learn, always in a rotten mood. She spent an inordinate number of hours preparing her briefings that took the form of slow lectures, and yet she always seemed in a rush.

With a wave of her hand, totally ignoring Peggy, she began. "Good afternoon, ladies, I am your supervisor on duty at La Guardia this month. I know all of you, with the exception of our new hire here – Ms. Shockley is an international hostess who was reassigned to help us with the new service we are inaugurating today on the St. Louis to Las Vegas flight. Welcome, Ms. Shockley." She nodded her head towards me. I smiled, mirroring Peggy's expression.

"Ladies, you will be the first to serve the 'Wines of the World' service. This service was designed to appeal to the wine connoisseurs who have requested a better quality of choices in the first-class cabin. Twelve bottles of premier French and Italian wines, in addition to your normal compliment of liquor, should be provisioned for first class. There should be nine red and three white, boarded by the St. Louis Commissary – make sure you get them before you depart. If there is a problem, you must contact a supervisor immediately. We have promoted this for weeks, and there can be no screw ups."

She went on to explain that the new meals included classic Chicken Kiev with saffron rice, medallions of pork complemented with sherry sauce and sage stuffing, and a six-ounce filet mignon with béarnaise sauce with a stuffed twice-baked potato. Based on the loads for the day, we should be provisioned with 20 percent chicken, 10 percent pork, and 70 percent steak.

She looked at me and smiled. "Additional linens will be boarded so that bread baskets will be linen-lined, and wine bottles wrapped to stop spillage on passengers' clothing, the same as on international."

I nodded my head in agreement. For the first time that day, I felt like I might know something. On TWA's international flights, everything in first class was linen lined. I figured TWA must have kept half of New York City's Finest Chinese laundries in business.

"Are there any questions?"

"Yes, are there any changes in coach?" one of the girls asked.

"Oh, yes, thanks for reminding me. We will be serving smaller splits of the same wine as is served in first class. The new entrée choices are chicken cordon bleu with wild rice, beef medallions in wine sauce with mashed potatoes, and pork with green beans, or something like that."

She searched her notes. Satisfied that we had all the information we needed, she became quiet. "Well, if there are no more questions, I must go. Enjoy your day and be safe." With that, she was gone.

"God, how I hate that woman!" Peggy said after she left. I waited for an explanation, but none came.

The flight to St. Louis was uneventful. While doing the emergency demonstration, I was amused with Peggy's announcements. Her opening line was "Good afternoon, ladies and newspapers," which caused the passengers to laugh, and I could feel the atmosphere transform into one of humor.

The flight whizzed by. Peggy was amiable and pleasant – when I dropped a full entrée on the floor, she calmly closed the galley curtain, bent over, picked up the contents and placed them back onto the plate, inspecting each one for items that may have attached themselves on the dirty galley floor.

Turning on her heel, she opened the curtain and delivered the entree to the unknowing passenger, who received extra attention later, just in case he suspected anything.

I soon discovered there were no extras and no time to rummage for leftovers on other trays like was done on international flights – you just made do.

The Las Vegas flight was very different. The passengers were not as serious as the previous ones. They classified as "TWAIPs," which translates into "TWA Important Passengers," and they seemed right at home – these men had flown over one million miles on TWA, and they deserved to be treated with respect.

They were also keenly aware of the new wine service; each carried a promotional page that had been included in their ticket jackets.

St. Louis Commissary had boarded 12 bottles of full-sized red and white wine for twelve passengers, along with the normal compliment of liquor; it was obvious that we had plenty of liquor for the three-hour flight.

It was a Friday night, so we instinctively knew that the passengers would be ready to let their hair down and get drunk. Most had already had a welcoming drink in the Ambassador Club, and a few seemed to be well on their way to inebriation. FAA regulations stated that we could not knowingly accept an intoxicated passenger on a flight, but these rules did not apply to TWAIPs, since our customer service supervisors, dressed in their flashy red coats, had personally escorted the men to their seats. They had no intention of addressing anything remotely familiar to an FAA directive; they just wanted them out of their hair as soon as possible.

As I looked down the first-class aisle, I saw twelve smartly dressed men beaming up at me. Like little children, they waited for their medicine. Each ordered a cocktail as they got visibly comfortable in their seats, loosening their ties and removing jackets, which we hung neatly. Unlike a true business group, newspapers and briefcases were noticeably missing.

They greedily sipped their cocktails and mentally undressed female passengers who made their way to coach. The men were feeling some-what haughty, as first-class passengers often do, watching the "peasants" jostle each other as they made their way to their confined and crowded seats in the back.

As I refreshed their glasses, I noticed that they seemed boldly familiar with one another. A partying mood had descended on the cabin, encouraged by Peggy's humor and inviting smiles. They began to laugh aloud as a group. This was a bad sign – familiarity is the breeding ground for rowdy passengers.

Peggy was truly in her element. She had revealed her love for Las Vegas layovers as we sat talking right after takeoff, and she said she was finally senior enough to fly it exclusively. I was impressed with her skills for remembering names – either she personally knew all these men or she had a great memory.

In fact, a little of each was true. She had a knack for names, and she admitted that she had flown with eight of the men previously. Either way, I was sorely impressed with the ease that she moved among the men.

After takeoff, as she began serving the hors d'oeuvres, I began opening the wine, so it could breathe.

My first bottle took an impossible amount of time to open. The cork was dry and very brittle, so I placed this bottle to the side and proceeded to try another. The result was the same for each of the twelve bottles – St. Louis Commissary had neglected to store the wine properly. I doubt that the corks had touched the wine since they left the factory winery in Europe.

I summoned Peggy to my side, behind the entry partition. "We have a problem." I whispered.

"Yeah, too many men and so little time!" she giggled deviously.

"No, I mean we have a big problem with the wine." It was then that she looked down and saw all twelve bottles lined up neatly on the floor by the boarding door.

"What's the problem? Are they bad?" She bent down and picked up a bottle, bringing the opening to her nose. "I drink Bourbon, so all wine smells bad to me." It was then that she noticed the cork boldly floating on the top.

"No, they're dry," I said. "I mean the corks are dry and brittle. I fought to get them open, and we now have cork floating in every single bottle."

"So what? They won't care. Look at how drunk they are!"

We both peeked around the corner to see one very aristocratic-looking male standing up and doing a version of the twist – and Chubby Checker he was not.

I began serving the entrees to the over-served men, as Peggy began pouring the cork-infested wine. It was not working – the first passenger to receive the wine was not pleased, and he began to slur and bellow loudly. "What's this in my 'Wines of the World' wine?"

Peggy swept the glass from his hand with a flourish and immediately returned to the forward door, where we had assembled a bar area.

"We've got to get this damn cork out!" she exclaimed breathlessly. "Maybe if we strained it through a napkin," I suggested.

I placed a napkin over the delicate wine glass. After what seemed like an eternity, the weight of the napkin caused the glass to tip over. The lackluster contents spilled onto the airplane floor, and the glass broke into small pieces. The napkin had been vigorously over-starched; it was impossibly non-porous.

Peggy whispered, "That will take forever. At the rate these guys are drinking, we'll never finish the service."

She stood in front of me with her hands on her hips, very deep in thought. Then suddenly, without a word, she turned and retrieved her crew kit from behind the last row in first class. Shouts came from the men as they complained about our lack of attention. Some knew we had a problem with the wine, but the news hadn't spread to the full cabin yet. I could hear her soothing them, but I could not make out what she was saying.

When she returned, she laid the crew kit on the floor. She retrieved a brand-new pair of pantyhose, still in the packaging. She opened it, laid part of it over the wine glass, and poured the wine through the hose. It filtered the cork as pretty as you please. We quickly poured twelve glasses and continued doing this until the passengers were satiated or just downright drunk.

Somewhere during this process, a man who was using the lavatory witnessed the creative wine-filtering process and grabbed the panty hose off the counter.

He waved the hose as he shouted to everyone, "She strained the wine through the crotch of her pantyhose!"

Laughter ensued, and I guess the rest was history. No amount of explanation could quell the visual of this statement. The men were so in love with Peggy, and so infatuated with the idea, that the truth never left the cabin.

Until of course, when the Orchid Letters came. We received twelve letters, all commending our creativity and professionalism.

My explanation of the events helped to contribute to the long, sometimes sordid and often misunderstood history of Peggy Iwanowski.

CHAPTER FIFTEEN

MEETING DIANA LYNN HALL

My father was stationed with the Army in El Paso, Texas in the 1940s. His wife - my mother - was a housewife and a dreamer. With little or no entertainment to provide an escape from the ramshackle military dwellings, she, like so many other stay-at-home wives, was enthralled by the many movie stars of the silver screen. Watching these entertainers would momentarily transport her away from the dirty, windy streets of a West Texas town to a world of glamour and beauty.

To supplement my dad's meager salary, she found a part-time job washing other people's dirty laundry in a local laundromat. But in her spare time, she would read the movie star magazines that profusely decorated the empty chairs. It was her entertainment until the clothes needed folding.

After the war, so many stars failed to climb the ladder to true stardom — one of those was Diana Lynn Hall.

An accomplished pianist, Ms. Hall had attained recognition as an actress, both on Broadway and in Hollywood. But after the war, along with many actresses, her bright star dimmed, and she was delegated to B-grade movies. But my mother adored her. So much so that when I was born, she named me after her.

My mother and I became estranged over the years, and my namesake and her story escaped my memory until one day in 1971.

Along with the rest of the flight crew, I listened as the Flight Service Manager briefed us on our upcoming flight to JFK from London. When he read the names of the TWAIPs ("TWA Important Passengers") that would be onboard our flight, one name startled me.

"Diana Lynn Hall," he read.

"Who's that?" one woman asked.

"I think she's a has-been movie star," someone else responded.

I recognized the name – was it really her? Until that moment, I had never truly associated myself with her, but she was real and alive and soon to be seated on my airplane.

The name brought up a suppressed memory of my mother scanning a *T.V. Guide*, hoping to find a movie that would prove Mrs. Hall's brilliance as an actress. She never found that movie, and I was left to conjure my own reality of her.

After completing the dinner service, I went to the First-Class cabin to find her. I wished my mother could be there – it would have been her "dream come true."

When I spotted Mrs. Hall seated in the oversized first-class seat, I was amazed at how tiny she was. She sat alone – dressed elegantly in a grey suit, so proper and graceful – staring out of the window. I approached her and introduced myself.

When I said my name, she stared at my name badge, which read Diana Lynn. Her eyes sparkled for a moment. I was unaware at the time that she was feeling unwell, and she invited me to sit, and we began to share our stories. I loved listening to her tell of how she rose from the ashes of WWII and became a star.

When I related, with affection, how much her portrayals of life meant to my mother, she began to cry. She shared that acting had meant so much to her and that fans, like my mother, were few and far between anymore.

I sat with her until I could see that she was beginning to tire. She took the time to write a quick note to my mother which read: *I've just met your lovely daughter Diana. What an honor to know that you named her after me. That was so sweet. Diana Lynn Hall.*

Ms. Hall died of a stroke soon after I met her.

TWA gave me many wonderful memories to share with my grandchildren, but how could anything surpass the meeting of a woman – a movie star, a legend in the eyes of my mother? Thank you, TWA.

CHAPTER SIXTEEN

MISTAKEN IDENTITY

They were the last two passengers to board the TWA 747, bound for London, England.

The Flight Service manager had received the final paperwork and was preparing to close the door when they appeared with the agent.

"I've added these two to the final count of 342 passengers," the gate agent said. "They just came running to the gate. They're lucky; they nearly missed it."

Breathlessly, the two men walked slowly through the crowded cabins, stopping occasionally to stare at the seat numbers overhead, and bumping into every seat that they passed.

The summer heat was exceptionally brutal in New York, and yet these two passengers were dressed in fatigues, caps, and matching heavy overcoats – the look was unquestionably early "Fidel."

Fresh in the minds of some fellow passengers were the recent hijackings to Cuba. José Marti Airport in Havana had become a popular destination for criminals unwilling to be prosecuted in the United States for their past crimes. Other hijackers just desired to see a paradise away from the U.S.A. The most recent hijacking was that of a Pan Am 747 – the hijacker's ticket was a pistol and a bottle of nitroglycerin. Fidel even visited the plane, musing over the questionable ability of the massive jet to takeoff on his short runway. The Pan Am pilot assured him that he would safely leave the island.

Perhaps these two men were unaware of the recent laws instituted by Cuba allowing Cuban immigration officials to decide the fate of the hijackers. Since it was almost impossible to tell whether a hijacker was a spy, the officials who dealt with them could interrogate them, beat them for information, and ultimately throw them into prison – for months.

One of the passengers was an older man, with a graying beard and mustache. With his considerable paunch, he was obviously someone who enjoyed the fruits of Cuban cooking. The other man was younger and smaller in stature, deferring to the older as they walked, offering his hand as a gesture of respect as he assisted when his older companion faltered.

I was standing in the aft cabin, taking my last meal orders. As they drew closer to me, I detected the aroma of garlic and cigars, laced with a very cheap aftershave. They tilted their heads and touched their caps as they walked past. When I stepped into a row to let them move past me, I noticed that the older man had a considerable bulge, covered up by his coat.

I watched as they passed the only two vacant seats. They proceeded to the very rear of the giant airplane, past the two lavatories and right into a closet. The closet was hidden by a curtain and designed to carry small cargo. They opened the curtain as if inspecting its contents.

As they turned and gazed quizzically at me, I pointed towards their seats. Together they returned to the two seats, in agreement. I smiled and shook my head "yes." As I continued to take meal orders, I watched them get settled, and was prepared to assist them if needed.

I was new to this. Having just graduated from the Academy months earlier, this wasn't my first time on a Boeing 747. However, since I was the junior hostess, I was awarded by default the E zone, known widely as the "drinking and smoking section."

Most of the airlines had followed United Airlines in designating smoking zones for passengers. The zones weren't really enforced, but it was an attempt at placating the non-smoking customer. (Never mind that the airplane recycled the same polluted air repeatedly.)

My attention was once again drawn to the men as they struggled to work their way into the small, Volkswagen-sized seats – the seats curved inward towards the rear of the plane, causing them to be difficult to access. As the older man fought to push his way into the row, I noticed him shifting the bulge in order to get into his seat. My curiosity was now piqued. *What could that possibly be?*

Fresh out of training, I was reflecting on a course called *"Profiling the Passenger and Knowing the Potential Threat."* The course syllabus, underwritten by the FBI, was designed to teach us to recognize the telltale signs of a hijacker.

Make verbal and visual contact with each passenger prior to the aircraft's departure. Look for signs of agitation, perspiration or irritation, the course had said. Grabbing two menus, I walked to over to the men. "Good afternoon, gentlemen. Welcome aboard."

They both looked up; the younger man smiled a toothless grin.

Handing them the menus, I said, "I'll be back in a moment to take your orders."

Neither had spoken, which made me think they probably didn't understand a thing I was saying.

Back in the galley, I asked my partner, "Does anyone speak Spanish?"

"You mean, the crew?"

"Yes, those two men don't understand a word of English. "

"I don't know, maybe the Service Manager would know?" she continued moving meals around in the massive galley.

Our zone was filled with an assortment of British citizens, American businessmen, and a sprinkling of elderly tourists. These two passengers obviously did not fit the assortment, and I had a nagging feeling that perhaps they were better suited for a National Airlines flight to Miami, but I had to believe that the gate agents had checked their passports and tickets.

A few moments passed and I returned to their seats to take their meal orders.

The younger man said in broken English, "We no eat." Then he handed the menus back to me.

"Sir," I said, "it's a very long flight. Are you sure you don't want to eat?"

Make light conversation with the passenger as you make eye contact. I looked intently into his eyes – they were bloodshot. Again, he said, "we not eat," as if he had it memorized.

The older man, meanwhile, had fished out the entire contents of the seat pocket in front of him, which he placed onto his opened tray table. He was sorting through the items, examining each one – or was he trying to cover something up?

I made a mental note to revisit the opened tray table since it needed to be closed before takeoff.

The younger man handed me the menus. "Would either of you like something to drink?" I asked. "A soft drink, or perhaps a beer – uh, *cerveza?" And they say I didn't learn any languages in California!*

The younger man smiled again, obviously impressed with my attempts at bridging the language gap. "No, thank you, señorita."

How odd, I thought. *This is a six-hour flight and they're not going to drink or eat.* Again, I pondered their reasons for flying to London.

I tallied my orders and returned to the galley, where my partner was moving entrées around in the ovens. "So, what are your two Cubans eating?" she muttered, extracting a pen from her mouth.

"How do you know they are Cubans?" I whispered.

"Dress code, my friend – they're following the dress code. Khakis, cap, and military jacket...check!"

"They aren't eating or drinking. Don't you find that strange on a six-hour flight?"

She smiled. "Not really. I bet they change their minds – I'll save two beef entrees for them. Don't forget to offer them headsets."

"I don't think they'll be interested in the movie, but I'll try later. Isn't it time for the demo? I need to get my stuff." I left the galley and walked to the back of the plane.

I had just reached my door and gathered my demo equipment when I heard the Flight Service Manager announce, "Arm your doors for departure."

I struggled to arm my door, kneeling to reassure myself I had done it right. As I stood, my attention was once again directed to the two men. The younger one was standing up and scanning the cabin.

Taking my emergency demonstration mask and life vest with me, I walked up to him.

"Sir, can I help you?" I asked.

Puzzled, he replied, "No, señorita, sorry. I was just looking at how 'largo' – eh, big – this airplane is. How many peoples does it carry?" He smiled – what teeth were left were brown.

"I'll tell you what," I said, I'll answer all of your questions – after you sit down and fasten your seat belt." I pointed to his seat.

He sat down, and I helped him find his belt, which he had, of course, sat on. I was nearly overwhelmed with the sour smell wafting from their unwashed bodies.

"Well, sir, each airline has a different passenger complement or number, but TWA carries 342 passengers and crew of 20," I answered hurriedly.

The older man, nodded, seeming to understand.

Pleased with the response, they smiled and looked down at the emergency placard that they had retrieved from the seat pocket in front of them.

"Well, I will talk to you later," I said. "Got to go to work." I continued up the aisle to begin the show.

As the Service Manager led us through the emergency procedures demonstration, the men's heads continually bobbed over the seats. They peered in rapt attention as I pointed out the location of the ten doors on the aircraft.

I finished off the demonstration with the jerk of the inflation handles on my life vest. The "Mae West" sprang to life with a loud hiss as the CO2 cartridges expelled their gasses – the kids loved this part. (We put fresh CO2 cartridges in daily to accentuate the real inflation of a life vest.)

Collecting my oxygen mask and dummy seat belt, I walked down the long cabin, checking each passenger's seatbelt and under-seat baggage.

The airplane taxied, smoothly and slowly. I took off my vest, trying to keep my bouffant hair bouffant. Once again, I smelled their unmistakable aroma – a tap on my shoulder confirmed the younger man standing behind me.

I was not happy with his sneak attack, and I am sure my face showed that. "Sir, you need to take your seat," I said. "We are on an active runway, preparing to takeoff." My heart was pounding. *Don't ever sneak up on me you smelly little creep*, I thought. *Now sit down before I knock you down.*

With a wave of his hand towards the front of the plane he asked me, "How do you get to the cockpit?"

"Do you mean me?" I asked, pointing to myself.

"No, me," he responded, walking back to his seat.

"You don't." I was thinking that we were as far from the cockpit as anyone on the plane.

"What do you mean, señorita?" He frowned as he sat down again, fumbling with his overused seatbelt.

I noticed that the other passengers were watching with a curious detachment. It was time for me to get serious and get this situation under control.

"Sir, I must insist that you stay in your seat." As I stood over him, he belted his seat belt once more.

"No one is allowed in the cockpit except our pilots. They stay locked in the cockpit the entire flight."

"But how can that be?" the older man questioned. "Do they not eat or use the toilet?" *Oh, and now he speaks English.*

I smiled confidently. "Well, of course they eat and use the bathroom. They have a bathroom near the cockpit and their food is delivered just as yours is."

The two passengers seemed content with this explanation. I, on the other hand, was starting to have suspicions about these two men.

Perhaps I was reacting to an incident that happened while I was in training. Two Cubans hijacked a National Airlines 727 to their homeland. They thought returning home in a shiny new airplane stolen from the USA would get them a little party with the big guy, Fidel. Instead, as the National Airlines jet opened its doors, the two men were whisked away in a black, shiny Chevy limousine, complete with armed guards.

The plane and its passengers returned home immediately after refueling. Fidel graciously ordered Cuban sandwiches and American Cokes to be distributed to the passengers. Instead of a "welcome home" party thrown at the palace, it seems the hijackers got a one-way ticket to prison with a "*not* getting out of jail" soon card.

The "what-ifs" hit me like a sledgehammer: *what if these two were planning to take MY airplane to visit Fidel? What was in the older man's pocket?*

The more I thought about all of it, the more I thought it might be a good time to share my anxiety with the captain. Looking out the window, I saw a large jet far ahead, pulling onto the active runway.

The captain was just beginning to speak over the public address system. Hearing his voice made me decide that it was time for a conversation with the man upstairs – and I wasn't thinking about God this time.

Not sure how much English these two understood, I walked to the airphone on the other side of the plane. My counterpart was on her knees talking to a cute man several rows ahead. *Sure*, I thought, *you get a date and I get two smelly guys who are going to hijack my plane.*

Picking up her phone, I searched in vain for the number to the cockpit. Eventually I resignedly pushed PP, which was like dialing 911.

Price Nations answered: "This is the engineer; may I help you?"

"Hi, this is Dianna at the R5 door. I have a possible situation back here."

"Have you spoken with the Service Manager?" He was following protocol, and I wasn't.

"I didn't think to call him. I'm sorry, was I supposed to call him?"

"Is it regarding a mechanical problem or a passenger?"

"Passengers, two passengers."

"Well, you should have probably called the Service Manager. Uh, just a moment, we're a little busy up here." *Oh thanks, Price, how about raising my anxiety level while you're at it?*

In the background, I could hear a distinct expletive. Then a cold voice spoke. "Captain Drake here. What can I help you with?"

"Sir, I have two suspicious-acting fellows back here that I am starting to get bad feelings about." *Shit I shouldn't have said "bad feelings," pilots hate the word feelings. They deal in facts – just the facts, ma'am, book 'em Dano…and all that.*

Direct and to the point, the manual stated. *Let the Captain have as many facts as possible and keep feelings out of it.*

"Explain 'suspicious.' Aren't you the new girl?" he asked.

Beads of perspiration slowly made their way down my back. "Yes, sir, I am the new girl."

"There are two men," I continued. "One older, one younger, both of Spanish or perhaps Cuban descent. They are dressed in combat fatigues with matching hats. They speak very little English, mostly Spanish, and they are asking many questions, like passenger loads and specifically how to get to the cockpit. They have not made any threatening advances, but they are making me uneasy. The older man has something very big and bulky in his pants, which is concealed with the jacket."

"I'll send the First Officer back. Meet him in the aft galley."

Hanging up, I made an even slower, deliberate walk to the galley. I prepared my best smile in order to mask the anxiety that was building inside of me. Immediately, I started to question my decision to call the cockpit.

Hoping I would see further evidence that these men were planning a new flight plan for my airplane, I slowed down and stopped near their seats, looking over their shoulders. Sure enough, they had the emergency placard in their lap, drawing with their nicotine-stained fingers what I decided were imaginary paths to the cockpit. *Shit.*

I continued my journey. As I entered the galley, the First Officer met me along with the Flight Service Manager and the Director of Customer Service (DCS).

"They are in 52E and 52F," I said.

"If those two are possible hijackers, I can't go back there and make myself a target. Captain Drake would have my head," the First Officer said.

"I'll go back," the Service Manager offered. "What am I looking for?"

The First Officer shrugged. "I don't know; anything suspicious, I guess."

The Service Manager began to walk through the cabin, making small talk with the other passengers as he worked his way back and around to the other side near my door. He peered over the seat to get a better glance at the two men, and it was then that the older man decided to move the bulky object in his pants. He stood up abruptly, obviously not bothered by the seat belt sign or the potential of the plane moving.

He adjusted whatever was in his pants, and, sensing he was being watched, he swiveled and looked right into the face of the Service Manager. Startled, the Service Manager turned and began walking back the way he came.

Watching the interaction, the First Officer said "How did we miss these two? They're a walking billboard for, 'Look at me, I'm a skyjacker!'"

"We have 342 people boarding – we can't stop every passenger with questionable dress and talk to them.," the DCS replied.

"They were the last two to board. It took them five minutes just to find their seats," I said quietly. The DCS glared at me.

"Then tell me who the hell is supposed to be profiling these people?"

The First Officer was getting more upset.

"We all are," the DCS said quietly, now realizing the potential problem.

Even if these men were totally innocent, the red flag had been raised. They would need to be checked; airline protocol insisted that any potential problem be resolved before a jet is allowed to depart.

Looking straight into my eyes, the first officer asked, "What have they said to you?"

"Nothing threatening really, just little questions like, 'How do you get to the cockpit?' and 'How many passengers does the plane hold?' Then there is the older man and his protruding bulge in his pocket," I replied.

"How big of a bulge?" the First Officer asked.

"I can't really tell since the fatigue jacket is so oversized, but it's at least as big as a bread box. I think their dress and mannerisms probably have as much to do with my concerns as their questions. But I'm the junior man here, I'll let you guys be the judge."

I was beginning to have my own doubts about my decision, but then the Service Manager entered the galley, out of breath and stuttering. "They are definitely up to something," he whispered. "There is something very big in the older man's pocket. Did you see him standing up?"

"Yeah, no accounting for stupidity," the First Officer said.

"He just stood up and moved something around in his pants pocket. Whatever it is, it is very large, but I couldn't tell because the jacket covers everything."

"Well, we can't take a chance," the First Officer said. "It looks like we're going to have to remove them. I'll go inform the captain."

"You can just remove people because they look suspicious?" the Flight Service Manager asked.

"Yes, we can, and we will. "Dianna, you return to your door, act normal."

Normal. Okay, and what would normal be at this moment? Walking past the two men, I again questioned whether I should have said anything. I was wondering how the company would go about firing me – I was on probation, so it would probably be neat and quick.

Right now, they looked like two unwashed men on their way to London, but what if they weren't? What if they were trying to be the second Cubans to catch the really big fish? The biggest prize for Fidel. The "Pregnant Guppy"!

My heart was racing. I barely heard the phone as it rang softly, red lights flashing an "all stations call." Picking up the phone, I said "R5," softly announcing my position. I heard all nine other positions report in on the line.

"This is Captain Drake. We have a situation on the airplane – we need to remove two questionable passengers from the rear of E zone. We will be taxing to an inactive runway, and the Port Authority team will use the portable stairs to extract two passengers. The R5 hostess is to disarm her door; all other doors will remain armed. Do you all understand? Dianna?"

"Yes sir." I replied.

"Ladies," he continued, "we are going to tell the passengers that we need to check a cargo door, so we will pull over to an inactive and have our mechanics look us over. Dianna, when you hear the knock, open the door – the first person will be a mechanic. After you point out the two men as discreetly as you can, move away to the other side. DO NOT ALARM ANYONE. Is this understood?"

As the Captain hung up, I saw a sky marshal whom I had met earlier at the briefing. He was partially hidden by the bulkhead wall, but he smiled at me and gave me a thumbs up. *Well, at least I have some support back here*, I thought.

The captain's voice came over the PA. "Good afternoon, ladies and gentlemen. It seems we have a little problem."

Groans could be heard throughout the large plane. The two men stuck their heads up and peered around, trying to understand what was happening.

"We have a warning light in our cargo bay sensors. In addition, another airline has confirmed that a cargo door seems ajar. We're just going to pull over here for a minute and let our mechanics look us over. I am sure we'll be on our way as soon as they check this out. Please remain seated, and we'll update you in a moment or two. Our hostesses will also remain seated."

Turning ever so slightly off the runway, it seemed like an eternity before our mammoth airplane finally rolled to a stop. The engines on the right side could be heard winding down.

My interphone rang again – this time the captain was calling for me only. "Dianna, disarm your door," he ordered. "Do it now."

I laid the interphone down on the top of my seat back, careful not to disconnect from the captain. I opened the cover to the door and moved the handle to the left, disengaging the slide. I reinserted a pin to make sure the door was disarmed. I also removed the red flag over the window to show anyone outside that the door was no longer armed.

I returned to the phone. "It is done, Sir."

"Good," he replied. "Did your buddies notice anything?"

The two men were looking out the window, deeply engrossed in conversation. I worried they might see the activity outside and become alarmed. "They don't seem to notice anything going on outside."

"Captain," I whispered, "should I keep the men occupied so they do not see anything out of the window?"

"They may see, but they won't suspect," the captain said. "The sky marshals have been informed and are ready to pounce if needed." I thought, this was his plane – he was ultimately responsible for everything that happened on it, so I would trust him.

Again, the older man started to get up. Reaching forward, I stood and tapped him on the shoulder. I made my best mean face as I shook my head. *No.*

Moments later, I could hear a sound outside my door – a series of slight bumps, followed by a loud knock. I stood up, silently peering out of my small window. I could only see diffused light, but I didn't need to know who it was. Rotating the arm of the massive door, I slowly tried to open it.

The 747 door was designed with a power assist mode, allowing anyone to open the 300-pound door with effortless ease. This was only engaged when armed, in an emergency, so I found myself fighting to push it open. From outside the door, a pair of very strong hands pulled as I pushed. When the door finally opened, a rush of hot, humid air slapped me in the face as the cooler air rushed past me.

The two men were now peering out of their window, unaware that this drama was all unfolding in their honor.

A man in a TWA mechanic's uniform stood outside the door, his uniform stretched over bulging muscles. "Where are they?" he asked.

"Right here," I whispered.

"Excellent." He smiled. "Make yourself invisible."

As the older man turned, he was looking into the eyes of the "mechanic." Another mechanic entered, as two men dressed in black uniforms stood on the narrow stairs to the door.

The group silently entered the cabin. Some passengers looked back to see the mechanics, but they didn't seem alarmed. The two men were involved with something in the seat that was keeping them occupied. *Probably setting the timer on their bomb*, I thought.

The police posing as mechanics placed their hands on the shoulders of each man from behind, quietly speaking to them in Spanish.

When they began to look in the overhead for their luggage, I came around the corner and said, "They didn't have anything other than the one bag."

The mechanic smiled, pointing his finger toward the corner where I was supposed to have remained.

As they walked by, the older man looked at me. I'm sure he was thinking – *all of this because I stood up too many times.*

The team quickly returned to the door with their charges. As silently as they arrived, they departed. Neither passenger spoke. It was as if they were used to being dragged off an airplane by 'burly Americanos.'

When I closed my door, I could hear the faint sound of the stairs being removed. It was over.

As I looked out the window and saw a fire truck glide past our aircraft, I was startled by a PA announcement. The captain explained that the cargo door was fine, and that as soon as he could restart the two right engines, we'd be on our way to London. I rearmed my door and felt a sigh of relief.

The passengers who had witnessed the extraction quietly chattered amongst themselves, but no one looked in my direction. I sat down and snapped my seatbelt, breathing a sigh of relief. Soon the calm voice of the captain announced that we were back on our way.

Weeks passed, and I was called to the Chief Hostess Office. She revealed that the two men were, in fact, Cubans who had participated in the annual "Viva Fidel" parade held in New York City. Due to a traffic jam, they were unable to change into more appropriate clothing. They also admitted to innocently sneaking a puppy to their niece who lived in London.

Oh well, you can never be too safe, right?

CHAPTER SEVENTEEN

FLIRTING WITH FIGHTER PILOTS

The Hotel Massimo d' Azeglio in Rome dates back to 1875. The exquisite lobby, designed to reflect the bygone opulence, was dark and cool, unlike the overheated, sunny day outside. Serene bellhops, their hands covered with white gloves, stand at attention, waiting for directions from their captain. They had been briefed earlier that today, like every other day, that buses would arrive with tired, disoriented tourists from America, passengers who would attempt to speak and ask them questions in English. The bellhops were to smile, not engage. Just smile.

Just as the bell captain promised, the lobby was being besieged by the boisterous passengers from my recent New York flight. An aircraft mechanical in New York had turned the scheduled nine-hour flight into a miserable twelve. The group, which was too numerous for the lobby, spilled out of the opened door, inviting in the noonday heat.

Two elderly men in wrinkled suits, puffing away on their overpowering cigars, laid claim to the only overstuffed chairs in the reception area. Their wives added to the cacophony, shouting at the desk clerks, attempting to speak Italian while jostling their Berlitz phrase books. The desk clerks, anxiously leaning across the marble counters of the check-in desk, attempted to quell the anxiety of the customers worried their reservations would not be honored due to the delay.

Suitcases, haphazardly strewn along the narrow entryway, eliminated any hope of escaping the fray. The older people pushed each other to get a better place in line – everyone wanted to see Rome before they died, and they were exhausted and angry.

Our replacement crew had just left for the airport, so our rooms were being cleaned. To escape the lobby, my crew chose to wait in the hotel restaurant where "special tea" was ordered, an airline code for semi-warm beer. My crew could not, of course, drink in uniform, so the beer was served in teacups. This "tea" helped to wind our bodies down after the long hours of serving passengers.

Nearly an hour later, as I reached my room, I saw a note on the floor. It read: *Hey Chick! It's me, Angela. I saw your name on the crew list. Get some sleep. Dinner? 6PM? Meet you downstairs.*

There is a fine line regarding sleep on international flights. Too much and you end up missing dinner, waking famished at 3:00 A.M. but unable to order food. The hours then slowly pass until breakfast, while you sit awake, reading and rereading the hotel menu.

If you get too little sleep before dinner, you then fight exhaustion, your eyes involuntarily closing. Four to five hours was an acceptable standard. The only issues were when shopping was thrown into the equation. It was always wise to take counsel from the more experienced senior hostesses, who had the entire formula down to a tried-and-true algorithm.

My hotel room was small and warm. Hotel rooms in Rome were not known for providing air conditioning, and this hotel, as luxurious as it was, was no exception. It did, however, have ornate drapes that covered the windows and helped to keep the brilliant summer sun at bay.

After a quick warm bath to relieve the sore muscles and tension, I fell onto the glorious cool sheets. The lingering effects of the "special tea" helped to send me into blissful, dreamless sleep. I was depending on the hotel's efficient wakeup service to jar me into reality four hours later. The thought of delicious Italian cuisine would help me to endure a quick cold shower to wake my body up, and I was excited to see Angela and show her what little I knew of Rome.

I found her seated in the baroque cocktail lounge, gin and tonics at the ready. After hugging, she said, "Can you believe this place? It's simply beautiful! I can't wait to walk down the streets."

I couldn't agree with her more. It was only my second time in Rome, but it felt like a dream – the buildings are so ancient, so historical. I hoped we could work the Coliseum into our plans that night – I wanted to visit the last time I was in town, but I had been too tired.

I told her that they had carriage rides with a tour guide, but Angela didn't seem too interested. I had learned that, unlike me, museums or tours bored her. Instead, we chatted about our trips and played a few hands of gin rummy. The bartender left a generous portion of olives and cheese as an appetizer. Our appetites piqued, we left for dinner.

The Scoglio Di Frisio Restaurant, with its fifty's atmosphere, was within walking distance of our hotel. Inside, you could close your eyes and imagine that you were a part of a Fellini movie, only in black and white, and it was popular among 747 airline crews because it could easily seat the entire crew of twenty together. When we entered, I felt confident that every hotel concierge within walking distance had mentioned this restaurant to their guests, as the place was packed with customers. It was noisy – elderly men and women strained to understand the waiters as local musicians serenaded loudly, collecting tips along the way.

Despite the crowd, Angela and I were seated at a table. "I'll order a carafe of Frescati," I said. "It's very refreshing. On my last layover here, I learned that Frescati is Rome's signature wine. It's been produced in the countryside surrounding the city by the locals for nearly 2,000 years."

"Oh goodness," she said, "you sound like a tour guide already! And hey, this is your party. I'll go with the flow."

As the waiter took our order, we noticed two extremely attractive men arriving. Both men were tan, fit and dressed like Americans – polo shirts and blue jeans.

"Fly boys," Angela quipped.

"Fly boys?" I asked. "How can you tell?"

"They're either commercial or military pilots. Check out the haircuts."

It had been rumored that air hostesses – a/k/a stewardesses – were party girls, dating all over the world. Well, not in our case – I hadn't participated in a real date since we graduated. We normally flew three days and then had two days off, and that's if we even secured a schedule. Not much time for dating.

Normally our first day home from Europe was spent sleeping, and our second was spent preparing for the next day, when we would fly again. We did get a stretch of time off – maybe four or five days a month – but that time was often spent flying home to see our families. If our roommates were home, we would occasionally go out together, but that was rare.

Meeting men wasn't a priority, particularly since time off didn't allow for a formal date. If a man in the states "happened" to be around and you happened to have the energy, there might be a date in your future, but most often, TWA found sneaky ways of messing that up. We were on reserve and at the whim of our schedulers.

"What do you think about the Coliseum carriage ride?" I asked.

Angela laughed. "That sort of sounds hokey."

"Maybe, but when will we ever be in the same place at the same time again?" I said.

"You're right," she agreed. "Is it expensive?"

"How would I know? I've never done it."

As we talked and laughed, another carafe of wine appeared. The waiter smiled and waved the pilots over. They had noticed us too, and the waiter commented that we were too beautiful to be alone.

Just as we had thought, they were Navy pilots stationed on the USS Constitution, located in the Mediterranean Sea. Steve was from Oregon and Bill was from Pittsburgh. Their jets were being repaired, so they only had the one night in Rome. Neither one knew what to order, so we suggested calamari and some other delicacies.

After we talked about our hometowns, the pilots asked the inevitable question.

"It's obvious why we're in Rome, but what are you two ladies doing here?" Bill asked, staring into Angela's blue eyes.

Angela loved this part of the game. "You guess," she replied.

Steve, the cuter one, thought we were American college students on a sabbatical. Angela, being 27 and long out of college, liked that answer a lot.

Bill, more Angela's style, guessed that we were with the Peace Corps. We kept this going for a while until we decided to reveal our occupation.

"Wow, now we can tell the guys on the ship that we had a date with a stewardess," said Bill.

"Uh, Bill, there's two of us," Angela quipped.

The reactions weren't new. In the new world order of 1970, a stewardess was akin to a movie star. Angela and I didn't understand this, but we didn't mind it, either.

After splitting the bill, we agreed to go and see the Coliseum together. Once we got there, we negotiated a fee for the four of us, and the buggy driver spoke enough English to make the tour worth the price.

The Coliseum, bathed in light, was a dream come true for all of us. This was a part of history that we were experiencing together. We sat quietly, imagining the Romans entertaining the crowd with the poor innocent animals and people alike.

Soon, however, our conversation turned again to food. Around midnight, not wanting the evening to end, we found a small café. We shared a pizza – had it not been for the constant badgering of the insistent streetwalkers, we could have been anywhere in the States, just four kids on a double date.

Steve and Bill asked us several times when our flight was departing – they were excited to see the 747 "up close and personal."

"I wish we could give you a tour." I said, "But I don't think that's possible."

Around 3:00 A.M., Angela and I left for our hotel. They both kissed us on the cheeks and pledged to write. We knew that would never happen, but we could dream.

The next morning, Angela and I met downstairs for breakfast.

"Those guys were so sweet," she said. "I think we all could have had a great time in New York. How old do you think they were?"

"What does it matter?" I said. "We'll never see them again. They're Navy pilots living on a ship, hanging out in the Mediterranean. They were cute, though."

Our crew bus came, and we both said goodbye to Rome, wondering how our "flyboys" were doing.

The heat of the day was replaced by the cool of the 747 cabin. The flight was full of anxious Americans, tired of calculating Italian currency and translating Italian words. They wanted a good old American hamburger with American beef, not that South America stuff. Time to go home.

We listened to the complainers, at the same time attempting to take meal orders and sell headsets before the door closed.

The passengers took longer than usual to board because of the frail, wheelchaired passengers. This gave us ample time to tally our meal counts and get our ovens loaded. We traded entrees with the "D" zone hostesses – they needed more chicken, and we needed more beef. Most of the time, it all worked out.

After performing our life vest demonstration, I walked back to my seat, preparing for a long 10-hour flight. As the 747 started lifting off the runway, the familiar drone of the Pratt and Whitney engines assured me that we were off successfully.

As I sat in my jumpseat, the phone near my head began to ring, startling me. I immediately thought there was an emergency, as using the phone on takeoff or landing was a no-no – the lines had to be kept clear in case of an emergency.

As I picked up, I heard the unmistakable voice of the captain: "Is this Dianna or Angela?"

"It's Dianna," I answered.

"Well, you and Angela make your way to the cockpit – pronto!"

"Yes sir." I hung up the phone. Struggling out of my seatbelt, I pondered this most unusual request. I walked to the other side of the 747 to alert Angela.

"We have to go to the cockpit right now," I said to her.

Angela's jaw dropped. "What? Why?"

"The captain just called and told us to get up there – now."

"But we haven't leveled out! We're still climbing!"

I grabbed her arm as she tried to wiggle free of her seat belt. "Let's go," I said.

Unexpectedly the captain's voice interrupted our trek: "Dianna and Angela, please proceed to the cockpit."

Making our way up the circular staircase in First Class, my calf muscles screamed. Finally, after climbing the stairs, I knocked on the door, which the engineer opened with a smile on his face. The cockpit was huge – it held five seats, conveniently arranged for the three man and two international relief officers, and it was filled with thousands of buttons.

Abruptly, the first officer removed his headset and handed it to me. Then the engineer handed Angela his headset.

"Ladies, take a seat. Put these on."

We managed to share the seat right behind the captain as we both put on their headsets.

"Now look out the windows, left and right," he ordered.

As we peered over the captain and first officer, he continued, "It seems you have a couple of pretty important friends that want to say goodbye."

And there they were: two Navy fighter jets, gears down, flaps down, all dirtied up, trying to slow down enough to cruise past us.

"Hello?" I said. "Steve?"

"Yes! Hey guys, we just wanted to say goodbye and thanks for the nice date," Steve said. "Tell your captain thanks, from one Navy man to another."

"Take care you two!" I managed to say. Angela never uttered a word. I'm not sure she even saw them.

With that, the two F-4's veered off and disappeared.

Nervously, I handed the pilots back their headsets.

Handing the headset to the first officer, the captain said, "You ladies must have made some impression."

As the 747 began an aggressive climb into the clouds, the captain turned his attention back to his controls. "Well ladies, I'll expect a full accounting later." That was our cue to leave.

We made our way back down the football field length of the plane, barely making out the captain's voice over the P.A. Much to our embarrassment, the passengers were clapping loudly. It seems he was bragging about our abilities to capture the hearts of the Navy.

This incident was never recalled or discussed in any airline circle. It seems several international air traffic rules were broken that day, but none by TWA.

CHAPTER EIGHTEEN

CELEBRITY STATUS

TWA was well known as the "Movie Star Airline." The status primarily came along with the notoriety of our famous owner, Howard Hughes who, in 1950 purchased RKO Studios and made a habit of dating the starlets that he met along the way. At that time his reported wealth was over $1.5 billion – which is $6.4 billion today. His wealth unseated oil magnates H.L. Hunt and J. Paul Getty for a time, but unfortunately, he was also unpredictable and unstable. His late-night phone calls to company president Jack Frye, along with other executives, were commonplace, as he wanted to discuss aircraft design changes. The employees of TWA referred to him only as 'the owner.' There were legendary stories that he would 'borrow' a scheduled airplane, as passengers lined up to board, to 'show off' for a movie star girlfriend.

It was true that every airline transported movie stars from time to time, but our New York to Los Angeles and New York to Las Vegas 747 flights were obvious choices for them, particularly in 1970 when the 747 was new and glamorous and *The Johnny Carson Show* was in its heyday.

On one particular flight from New York to Las Vegas, I had showstoppers Bill Cosby, Minnie Pearl, and Don Knotts, all seated near each other in the large First-Class section of the 747. There were plenty of memorable comments between them when we hit some severe turbulence. I recall Bill Cosby shouting, "If this plane goes down, I get top billing!"

I was shocked when after landing in Indianapolis, our captain informed me that Arnold Palmer had just parked his jet next to ours, and that he would be boarding any minute. He was a well-known pilot as well as an accomplished golfer, and in a moment, there he was: all tanned up, with his white hair poking out of his PGA cap. He announced that he was on his way to Honolulu for a planned tournament, and he spent several minutes in the cockpit chatting up our crew.

We always made sure a group of coach seats was blocked when Joey Heatherton was scheduled to return from L.A. for some much-needed sleep after her late-night performances – she often flew home to see her parents in New Jersey. She always seemed a little grumpy – which we attributed to fatigue – and she never drank, nor ate. She just slept as we kept the public at bay.

Cary Grant boarded our flight from JFK to LAX. He drank a little too much and then asked us to join him at his home. It seems his wife, Barbara Harris, was out of town, and so he invited the entire crew to join him to watch the Super Bowl. We sadly declined.

We all sang, "God Bless the U.S.A" with Lee Greenwood as he deplaned in L.A. He was unknown at the time, but he soon achieved fame after the song was previewed on an episode of *The Tonight Show with Johnny Carson*.

Natalie Wood and Richard Wagner sat in our First-Class cabin from New York to Los Angeles. She never spoke, and he made her personal requests known to us. They were a beautiful couple, and she was especially radiant when she smiled.

Of course, I met Clint Eastwood in the beginning of my career and my namesake Diana Lynn Hall later on.

Long before they splashed onto the music scene, a band named Earth, Wind and Fire booked reservations in the rear of our Boeing 707 at the last minute, only because the jet they had chartered experienced engine problems. They were a very diverse group of young men who flirted with us incessantly. I was in awe – I had never met a real, live band before.

Tom Jones flew from New York to London on our 747, and he invited us all to come backstage at his show, where he would be singing his newest song, "What's New Pussycat?" I was very junior at the time, and as usual, the more senior girls went, leaving us behind in our hotel rooms.

I was privileged to see and speak with Audrey Hepburn as she flew from Zurich to New York. A special meal was ordered for her – all fresh fruits. She ate so little of it, drinking only Evian water and sleeping the entire flight. Her appearance was shocking and sad – she was so tiny and frail. We were unaware of her battle with stomach cancer at the time.

Ray Bolger, better known as the Tin Man in *The Wizard of Oz*, was affable and gracious, even after I admitted that I had never seen the movie. He asked how that could be, and I explained that my religion didn't allow movies. He was baffled. I made a conscious effort to watch his movie afterward.

I was tasked with personally watching Tatum O'Neal as she traveled between her parents in L.A. and New York. She and I had met one fateful day when our plane took a long delay in New York and her stepmom, Joanna Moore, had already left for home. Tatum had just won an Oscar, and at only 10 years old, she was very precocious. We became fast friends as I tried to keep pace with her on the airplane. (All unaccompanied minors were very special and required attention from all of us, and we tried to keep them busy and well-fed (– a packet of toys and games was loaded onboard each plane just for them.)

When we arrived in L.A., I was met by Ryan O'Neil himself. He was sweet and obviously was a loving father. I flew with her several more times after that.

Gina Lollobrigida sat in First Class from Rome to New York. When I walked by her, she touched my smock and asked for a drink of water. When I returned with the water, her handler, who was just returning from the lavatory, chastised me for 'bothering' her. She graciously defended me and offered me an autograph. I was the only one on board who got one of those that day; I have to say she was very gracious and very beautiful.

Every retired and active flight attendant has stories to match mine, but this one story remains mysterious and quizzical:

Flying from La Guardia to Chicago on a 727, there were over 30 Orthodox rabbis who had boarded in my coach cabin. One man in particular sat alone in the first row of coach, and his party hovered near him as if to protect him. When dinner was served, I began to approach him with his kosher meal, but I was immediately rebuffed by a particularly large rabbi.

"You must not touch nor speak with him," the large man said. I gave the meal to the protector and resumed my duties in First Class.

When we arrived at the gate, the jetway was overrun by men and women waiting for the famous rabbi. As the gate agent attempted to open the door, it was impossible. After what seemed like an eternity, several Chicago police pushed their way through the crowd. We threatened to keep everyone, including the rabbi, on-board if the crowd didn't disperse. After the regular passengers deplaned, he was allowed off the aircraft.

Later we speculated that possibly the rabbi was there to boost the Jewish community during the Skokie trials, because of the neo-Nazis' decision to march on the city where so many Holocaust victims resided.

CHAPTER NINETEEN

HENRY, THE HESITANT HIJACKER

The day at La Guardia had not started off well. Storm clouds gathered outside as delays caused by a stalled weather front around New York created a small tsunami of angry passengers who wandered aimlessly in search for answers to their particular situations. Overhead, announcements played continuously, explaining the reason for the delays, but they were ignored. Only face-to-face confrontations would do. Airline employees, regardless of their job descriptions, were fair game – the gate agents took the brunt of the abuse.

Flight crews found little solace. The crew lounges, normally an escape from the fray upstairs, were not known for their amenities, and on a day like today they were full. The small TWA crew lounge had a few old couches with protruding springs, but they were always covered with mysterious-smelling airline blankets procured and accumulated over the years by flight crews. There was always someone attempting or pretending to sleep, and a few chairs offered opportunities to sit and read — if only there could be light. We could fix a broken airplane, but finding a lightbulb for a reading light in the crew lounge was impossible. The rooms, as uncomfortable as they were, did offer a place to escape the maddening pace of the world upstairs – sanity had its price.

In search of extra quiet, I decided to go and wait on my delayed airplane instead. It offered me the peace and silence that I longed for, and it was easily accessible – a short walk down the stairs, past operations, and then through the open 727 aft stair, which had been left open to help balance an otherwise empty airplane.

The overhead lights on the plane were on. They were being powered by a GPU – a ground power unit. Although there was little air flowing through the partially closed air vents, it felt peaceful. I opened my book and breathed in the quiet.

I smelled him before I saw him. His breath was hideous.

As I turned, I was confronted by a tall, unshaven man. He was at least six feet tall, with a muscular build, and his blue eyes were reddened. He appeared wild but his voice was calm – he was tired, lacking emotion. His left hand tensed around my shoulder as he raised me out of the first-class seat. The cold of a gun chilled my skin as it brushed past my arm.

What is he doing here? How did he get onto the plane?

Finally, he spoke, slurring his words. "So, how's about a little ride to Las Vegas, missy?"

Probably drunk, I thought. His grip was tight and solid – there would be no winning this fight if it came to that. He turned slightly as he stared down the long rows of empty seats, the silence seemed to go on forever. The cabin lights were off and cabin air was flowing at a minimum.

"Where are the rest of your airline buddies? How come it's so dark and hot in here?" he commanded, wrestling with his shirt collar. I knew I should be afraid, but somehow, he was unconvincing. He betrayed his unpremeditated plan.

The only sound in the cabin was the constant drone of the GPU. I suddenly longed for the throngs of passengers that I had avoided just moments before.

"Sorry I yelled," he said, with unexpected kindness.

Today of all days, I had tried to escape the crazies upstairs, and here I was with a bona fide one. "I'm the only one here," I mumbled as I looked around, hoping I was wrong just this one time.

"So, isn't this the airplane to Las Vegas?" He was breathing faster now. "Where are they?"

"Who's they?" I asked, knowing the answer but stalling all the while.

"You know, they – THE PILOTS," he shouted again, in a half-attempt to scare me. It didn't work – my childhood was filled with fearful moments; I was immune.

"Well, actually, I don't know where they are. Our scheduled departure is on hold due to the weather." I managed a half-smile.

His eyes again wandered down the long, empty aisle. Normally filled with passengers, an airplane can be very lonely when it's empty. He giggled, and the giggle made me wonder if this guy was a mental patient or perhaps high on drugs. I could feel the gun poking in my ribs.

The gun. Had I actually seen a gun? The chances of a rescue were very small, since the airplane had been cleaned and serviced before I boarded. Any amount of time might pass before my crew or someone from the ramp might appear. This guy could do just about anything to me and no one would know. How ironic my solitude might be my undoing.

My hijack training was sitting right in the back of my brain, beeping: *Ready to access information? Assess the situation. Protect your passengers.*

The hijack training class was one class that I had particularly liked. It seemed as if many years had passed since then.

There were no passengers, so I was next on the list to protect.

Beep, more information. Assess the danger. Make the hijacker reveal his weapon or item of threat.

I tried to look down by my waist, but his jacket concealed what it was he had poking into my side. He stared coldly into my eyes, and I decided that it would be better to wait on that.

Beep, next step please. Engage hijacker in conversation. Get to the reason for attempting to take your plane.

The class had been taught by a former FBI agent, which I had always found a little fishy. He had seemed so young – how did you become a former FBI agent at such a young age? Does that translate into a *fired* FBI agent?

My mind was now working overtime, and it felt as if time had slowed down. I noticed beads of sweat starting to form on his brow. *Dear hijacker,* I thought, *please be advised that the Ground Power Unit will be operating at a minimum. Your cabin temperature will not be regulated to suit your needs, asshole.*

Maybe he was losing his grip on his ill-advised plan. "Look," I said. "I could lie to you and tell you that my crew is on their way, but the truth is, this plane isn't scheduled to go anywhere for hours."

"So, you're telling me that I am trying to hijack a plane that has no crew and no passengers and isn't going anywhere?"

"Yes, that's about it."

"So, if that's true, what are you doing here?"

"I needed a quiet place to read my book. This was the quietest place I could find. I might ask the same of you."

"What?"

"What are you doing here? You just don't look like the face that might grace a post office billboard."

"I'm trying to find a quick and easy way to Las Vegas!" He scowled.

Ah, a little anger there. Reality must be creeping in on his little plan.

"So, this might sound stupid, but have you tried buying a plane ticket? It's a lot less risky," I suggested.

He didn't reply, so I continued: "Do you have any idea how much trouble you're in? And that's before you even complete your job...of hijacking, that is."

He looked straight at me. "Well, I'm not planning on killing anyone. And all I want to do is go to Las Vegas."

"But hijacking is a federal crime. Prison...Leavenworth...the Big House. Plus, let's talk about your chances of even doing this. Do you honestly think that TWA is going to put passengers and crew on board so you can hijack them?"

I hoped that this revelation wouldn't send him over the edge. With this information, his shoulders slumped noticeably, and he sat clumsily into the seat. His grasp on my waist caused me to follow him into the adjoining seat. Something fell onto the floor. It was then that I saw the weapon: a small gray plastic gun. A toy!

I pulled myself up and stood over him. He looked as if he was going to cry. A smile ran across my face. "You know that's a toy gun you have there?" I asked.

"Yes, I know. It's all I could find on such short notice." He buried his face into his hands.

I was using everything in my power to suppress the laughter that had replaced the subsiding panic.

"I'm just curious," I said. "How did you think you were going to hijack a plane with a toy gun? We would have eventually asked to see your weapon. We're professionals; we know a toy gun when we see one." I wasn't afraid anymore – now I was getting angry.

"I was hoping that I could keep it hidden. It's my nephew's; I took it out of his toy box after my bachelor party ended this morning."

"You came from your bachelor party to hijack a plane?" I could detect the beginning of a giggle from deep within my chest.

"Yes, I was at my bachelor party last night. You got a problem with that?"

"Yes, I actually do have a problem with that!"

"Oh, my God, I've really screwed this up this time! She's never going to marry me." His face was turning redder by the second, and he was starting to cry.

"Wait, don't cry." I couldn't believe I said that.

For the first time, I really looked at him. Damn, this guy was handsome. Even though they were reddened, his eyes were deep blue. His hair was black, and he had a cleft chin, sort of like Clark Gable's. Stubble was more obvious now in the light, and his clothes were clean but obviously slept in – a pizza stain had spoiled his once-pressed and starched shirt. I could easily have dated this guy – if he hadn't thought about taking my plane to Las Vegas.

As I stood over him, his head in his hands, I felt an overwhelming sense of compassion. Tears lined the man's face as he reached down under the seat, grabbed the toy gun, and, after a second, handed it to me.

"I'm not a violent man," he said. "I'm really sorry if I scared you. I just need to get to Las Vegas. I was supposed to catch a flight there last night – you know, the red-eye. I was getting married today." He was beginning to gain control of his emotions again.

"Are you getting married?"

"What do you mean?" he asked.

"So what's stopping you, other than the weather?"

"I got drunk and missed the flight. I also misplaced my ticket and my wallet. My wedding is at 4:00 P.M. today, in Las Vegas."

"Okay, so that's your reason to hijack a plane?" I was incredulous.

"Hey, it's all I could come up with at the moment, okay? Anyway, I think the gin may have helped."

"What's your name?" I offered my hand to shake. "My name is Dianna."

"Henry, Henry Van Court." He stretched his hand out to mine. He had soft hands and well-manicured nails – by the cut of the Armani suit, I guessed he was an accountant or an attorney, maybe even a doctor.

Sitting down in the seat across the aisle from him, I said, "Henry, you don't seem like the kind of guy to even consider hijacking an airplane. Why don't you just call her and work this out?"

"Dianna – may I call you that? – this is the second time that I have done something to delay this marriage. The last thing she told me was, 'If you screw this up again, it's over.'"

"Oh, she'll forgive you. We always do."

"No, she won't forgive me this time. Her parents are in Las Vegas – her dad is my boss – and they aren't real keen on me, so this will be the final screw up. I will lose my job and my future wife."

"And what did you do the other time, if I may ask?"

"I just didn't show. That was two years ago. I faked an appendicitis attack," he admitted. "It's my friends – they manage to talk me into walking away, but later, over time, I regret it."

"You can't blame it on other people," I said. "In the end, it's your decision."

We sat in silence, as memories flooded into my brain. I wondered how my life might have changed if only my beloved had made a different choice. If only he realized that we were meant to be married. But were we? These questions had been revisited multiple times with no resolution. In this moment, however, I had a chance to help this man make the right decision.

"Give me the details of your wedding."

"I am supposed to be at the chapel by 3:00 P.M. The wedding is at 4:00."

"Henry, do you know what time it is in Las Vegas?" I asked. "It's only 7:00 A.M. here, so it's 4:00 A.M. in Vegas – we've got loads of time to get you there! We need to call those so-called friends, get them out of bed. They can buy you a new ticket."

"What do you mean? There's no way, is there? I mean, could you?" He was stuttering now and standing. His whole demeanor had changed. He looked at me. "But I tried to hijack you."

I stood too, looking down on him with a hand on his shoulder. "Well, I'd hardly call that a hijacking attempt," I said. "I don't think you ever got around to actually saying the word 'hijack.' As far as I could tell, you were lost, a little intoxicated, and looking for the flight you missed last night. You saw me, fell in love, and followed me to my airplane. We can leave out the toy gun part – it will save me years of embarrassing jokes from my peers, and prison time for you. I have to say, you were pretty unconvincing as hijackers go." I started to really smile for the first time.

"Are you sure?" he asked. "I mean how do you know?"

"Look, Henry, I've haven't been hijacked before, but I'm pretty sure what you did wasn't enough to get you on the FBI's Most Wanted List. You need to get some training if you want to pull this off successfully."

"No, I meant the part about getting to the wedding on time and the ticket and everything?" he sputtered.

"Braniff has a nonstop leaving in about four hours. By then, this weather should have cleared."

"You're not going to call the police?" he asked, astonished.

"No, not today," I replied, "We'll just keep this between you and me."

He couldn't believe his ears – he wasn't going to jail, and he might get to Vegas on time. "Why are you doing this for me?" he asked. "I mean, can't you get into trouble for not turning me in?"

"Not turning you in for what? I've already forgotten." I smiled. "By the way, just for the record, how did you get on my plane?"

"It was pretty easy. I watched you walk on the plane from up there." He pointed up at the large plate glass windows that lined the airport ramp. "I had been in the airport all night, and when I saw how easy it would be to get on the plane, I went for it." He smiled.

I realized that any passenger could view the activities of crew members through the large plate glass windows. He must have seen me board the airplane through the aft stair.

"But, how did you get downstairs, through the doors, Henry?" Those doors required a code that only airline crew knew.

"I just walked in behind a couple of pilots. They were talking. They never even asked what I was doing down here."

That sounded about right. Crews were accustomed to men who looked like they had been sleeping in their clothes all night. He certainly fit the description of a commuting pilot.

I chuckled to myself. *This report will be interesting.* But wait, I couldn't tell the company because I had no intention of having this man arrested for trying to get to his wedding on time. *Oh well, this will be one for that book that I'll write someday.*

"Are you ready to start this adventure?" I extended my hand as I smiled at Henry.

"Yes, I guess I am." He smiled back.

About a month later, I received a package in my crew mailbox. Inside was a photo of Henry and his new wife. He was radiant, and she of course, was as beautiful as I expected. A note read, "Thank you, Dianna, for turning my day around. Love, Henry and Jennifer."

I will admit that I cried, knowing that were it not for my interference, their lives would have been different. God does work in mysterious ways.

CHAPTER TWENTY

STAR WITNESS

As the Boeing 727 turned from the active runway and taxied towards the terminal at La Guardia, we had just finished serving the breakfast service. During that time, a particularly handsome man had asked if I'd like to "do lunch."

Now, I had a rule about dating passengers – "rarely, if ever" was the rule, and never with pilots, who were always married, no matter what they told you. When I saw this man board my plane in Dayton, Ohio, however, I knew that my rule was about to change. Tall, dark, and handsome perfectly described this absolutely gorgeous man. His business card – which he dropped on his used breakfast tray – declared that *"Maverick is back and ready."* He worked for the Ford Modeling Agency, and I was intrigued. After a brief chat, we agreed that Smith and Wollensky's, at 3rd and 49th in Manhattan, would be the perfect first place to enjoy each other's company and a perfectly cooked steak.

As the plane parked at the gate, I heard three bells over the P.A. Picking up the phone in the rear of the plane, I heard Jeanine, who was working First Class, quickly announce that a supervisor was on the jetway. It was a warning: the supervisor was obviously there for a reason. Rarely did one meet a flight to deliver messages to passengers – that was the duty of a gate agent – so the supervisor was looking for one of us.

My thoughts went to my family in L.A. Hopefully it wasn't bad news.

As the front door opened, Jeanine then identified the familiar face of Supervisor Osborn, who was accompanied by two men in brown overcoats.

Again, the phone rang, and I answered. "The wicked witch Osborne is here," Jeanine said. "Looks like the cops are with her. Did you rob a bank or something?"

Then I heard Ms. Osborne's unmistakable voice as she wrestled the phone away: "Ms. Shockley, please gather your things and meet me at the jetway."

As I began my walk down the now empty cabin, I was reminded that my hair was no longer pinned up. Even though the flight was over, my derelict hair was in clear violation of the TWA grooming policy. I had taken it down to impress my lunch date, but not wishing to engage with the intolerant supervisor, I quickly repined it.

As I reached the front door, Ms. Osborne introduced me to Detectives Petroski and O'Leary from the Jersey City Police.

I felt uneasy and tried to recall if I'd ever broken the law. They both smiled at me to ease my obvious uncertainty about their reason for meeting my flight.

Detective O'Leary leaned forward. "Can you give us a few minutes of your time to answer some questions?"

"Of course," I said. "Will it take a lot of time?" I was thinking of my lunch date with Maverick.

Before they could speak, Ms. Osborne interrupted, her eyes intense: "Dianna, this is a police matter. You will stay as long as it takes."

"Will I get to make a phone call?" I asked.

"You're not under arrest!" Detective Petroski replied, laughingly. "Of course, you can make a phone call later."

As we left the plane on our way downstairs, I saw Maverick standing ahead of me, just outside the airport door. He had lingered – curious, I suppose, if I was going to be hauled off in handcuffs.

"Excuse me, gentlemen, I need to speak with a friend."

They both smiled. Ms. Osborne looked like she was going to scream.

When I caught up to Maverick, he turned and whispered, "Is everything okay?"

"Yes, but I think we'll need to cancel our date today."

He looked at the men and laughed. "Too many parking tickets?"

"Actually, I don't know yet what's going on." I giggled. "And I don't own a car. How did you know they were cops?"

"It's instinctive. Call me when this is over, unless they put you in the big house!" He laughed.

"Very funny."

He reached over and kissed me on the cheek. *Smells good, looks good, laughs at my calamity – I think I'm in love.*

When I returned, the two police officers were chatting with Ms. Osborne. She took us down the jetway to her office. Hoping to get in on the action, she was instead rebuffed by Detective O'Leary. "Thank you, ma'am, we'll call you if we need you," he said, and closed the door.

Smiling, he took a seat. "I guess you are curious about why we are detaining you?"

"Yes. I don't recall breaking the law." I giggled nervously.

"Have you ever been arrested?" Officer Petroski asked, his face pensive and somewhat scary.

Before I could answer, they both burst into laughter. The antiperspirant that had promised to keep me dry under any circumstances failed, and I finally began to get frightened.

Detective O'Leary reached over to touch my shoulder saying, "We're sorry about that; I apologize. It's rare that we talk to upstanding citizens. We just needed a little humor. It brightens our day."

"Take a seat," Detective Petroski said, pointing to Ms. Osborne's office chair.

When I did so, he continued: "We are with the Jersey City Homicide Division. And this is most certainly not about you – we are conducting an investigation regarding a homicide that happened in our city a few months ago. Two brothers murdered an innocent man on our streets. You may have encountered one of the shooters unknowingly."

Where could I have encountered a killer? I thought.

Detective O'Leary carefully laid five photographs on the desk.

"I want you to look carefully at these photos," he said, "and tell me if you have ever seen any of these men in the last few months."

Now I hate to quote the old saying that "all black men look alike." Black or white, it doesn't matter – I was very nervous about staring at photos and picking out a man I *might* have seen months before and who might just be a *killer.*

Before I looked at the photos, I asked, "Can you give me a little more information?"

Detective O'Leary looked at his notes and said, "Do you recall flying to San Francisco on Flight 43 on February 20?"

"I guess I must have if you are here questioning me." My brain was now working overtime: *Do these two cops honestly think I can identify a passenger from a flight, months, weeks, or even days ago?*

"Let me see if I put anything in my flight log," I said. "I keep notes on my flights, and perhaps there's something in there that will help me recall. Hang on, let me look."

As I fumbled for my logbook, Detective Petroski watched me intently. I managed to locate the date in my logbook, and I read my notes aloud: "Flight 43, JFK to SFO, worked C, 60 peeps, strange pax, didn't eat, didn't sleep, no free movie, refused to spread out."

"Now in English, please." Detective O'Leary said.

"I was working the aisle, which is the (C) position. It was a seven-hour flight plan. We had head winds, which added an hour to the usual six hours. The cabin was practically empty, and –?"

Suddenly, a memory came to mind. "There was a strange passenger," I continued. "He was very quiet, very pensive. The first thing I noticed was his green simulated leather jacket, which I offered to place overhead.

I don't usually offer to put a passenger's items in the overhead, but he seemed confused or scared. He was sitting in the center seat, which I found odd, since there was no one on either side of him, but he refused to move. He never ate, never slept. He didn't want to watch the movie. Honestly, I doubt that he used the lavatory. I remember I had to hide his meal from my partners in case he changed his mind about eating."

"You hid his meal? Why?" Detective O'Leary giggled.

"The other hostesses would have eaten it. We are always hungry, and it was a very long flight."

Looking back at the photos of faces, I asked, "Do you know which seat he sat in?"

They smiled. "Do you?" Detective Petroski asked.

I realized that I did know. "Yes. It was 21E."

Both officers now betrayed their cool – they smiled and became more animated. "Can you look at these photos and see if you can recall his face?" Detective O'Leary asked.

Realizing the seriousness of my situation, I carefully picked up each photo and encouraged my memory to kick into high gear. As I stared at the faces, two seemed to share a family resemblance. After a very long moment, I handed one of the photos to the officer.

I had successfully identified one of the killers.

"You said they were brothers, right?" I asked.

"Yes," Detective O'Leary said.

Handing another photo to him, I said, "Well, I think this must be the brother."

Both detectives smiled and gave a thumbs up.

"You are amazing." Detective O'Leary said. "Just one more request. We need you to accompany us to make a positive ID. It seems our perp was caught in someone's home without permission, and he's being arraigned today for burglary. We're hoping with your help, we can get him held over for questioning."

"Where are we going?" I asked.

Detective Petroski picked up the photos as he answered. "We're going to the Jersey City Municipal Court. It's about an hour from here. Help us out and we'll buy you lunch."

"At Smith and Wollensky's?"

"Well, that's pretty ritzy for our budget, but we'll check it out," Detective O'Leary said.

"I'm sorry, I was just kidding," I said. "Wait, will he see me?"

"I doubt it – we will be seated in the back of a very busy courtroom. But just in case, we'll lend you one of our super-duper overcoats to cover that lovely uniform." I could tell Detective O'Leary was trying to reassure me.

The car was an older model – not exactly an exciting ride to the courthouse. No lights or sirens, only seats loaded with used coffee cups, food wrappers, and old newspapers. As Detective Petroski attempted to tidy up before I got in, I spotted a half-filled crossword puzzle on the driver's seat.

"Sorry, we've been living in this car for a month. We're not very neat," he said. *Well, that is an understatement.*

As we entered the parkway, the traffic slowed down.

"So, do you like your job?" Detective O'Leary asked.

"Yes, I love my job," I answered.

"Really? What's the best part?" He grinned.

"Getting to meet real cops." I laughed, and so did they.

The Jersey City courthouse was a large limestone building with wide steps that led inside. People milled around outside, smoking and waiting for their turn to appear before the judges inside. As we entered the building, we were met by two uniformed police officers.

I was now wearing O'Leary's wrinkled and stained overcoat. "Your coat looks better on her than it does on you," one of the patrol officers commented curtly.

"Observant, don't you think, Ms. Shockley?" O'Leary said. "Yes, our police department is filled with keenly observant and hilariously funny guys." He leered at the patrol officer, who immediately disappeared.

Petroski had explained that we would be entering a courtroom filled with petty criminals, all awaiting decisions from the judge based on the evidence provided by their court-appointed defenders. They'd either be fined or held over for trial.

After peering into the room, we entered from a side door and made our way towards our seats. People in an assortment of dress stared at us as we did so. I was very uncomfortable, and my heart began to race. *What if he recognizes me? Will he remember me from so many months ago? Will I recognize him?*

Soon I was squeezed in between the two cops on a row of seats occupied by some very interesting-looking people. O'Leary and Petroski had insisted on sitting in the middle of the row, having spotted three magically vacant seats in the middle of a full courtroom. On either side of them sat two more police officers, who greeted us.

"Hear ye, hear ye Court, the honorable Judge Meyer is now presiding," the bailiff announced.

We all stood as a short, overweight man with a red face and a mane of white hair walked into the courtroom and took his seat.

"You may be seated. Court is now in session," the bailiff shouted again.

"We'd like to call Ronnie Chaney," the prosecutor said, staring into the crowd.

As my eyes scanned the room, the man in front of me turned briefly and I got a look at his face. I couldn't believe it – as he pushed his way to the front of the crowd, he even had on the same green jacket.

I grabbed O'Leary's hand in a death grip. I didn't make a sound, fearing Ronnie Chaney might turn and see me. We stood quietly and left the room.

Outside of the courtroom, I tried to catch my breath. "That's him," I whispered, in a throaty, silent whisper.

"Are you sure?" O'Leary asked.

"Positive."

My ride back to Manhattan was filled with a discussion about what would come next. The detectives explained that the brothers, who were twins, had planned the execution of a man as he left his dry-cleaning business. Both brothers had been arrested and declared that they were not present at the shooting.

To establish an alibi, one brother – Johnnie, the shooter – hid out with a relative, while Ronnie, the other brother, purchased a ticket on my flight. Their plans unraveled, however, when the homicide squad began to piece together the facts.

Detective O'Leary had questioned all the TWA employees associated with his flight, as well as all the agents and inflight hostesses, and I was the only one who had identified the shooter.

I was relieved to know that my participation was minimal until the murder trial began. I was told that months – maybe years later – I would be contacted again by the police, and at trial I would be their "Star Witness." For the first time, I realized how scary my small part in this drama had become. What if the killers tracked me down? I wanted to believe that TWA would protect my identity, but now I realized that this day had most likely changed my life forever.

I declined lunch and was soon deposited at my door.

"Nice looking dates," my roommate Angela commented as they left. "Do I get the fat one or the bald headed one?"

CHAPTER TWENTY-ONE

THE BIGGEST LITTLE AIRLINE IN THE STATE OF TEXAS

On a bright summer day in 1970, our 747 lightly touched down on a massive runway in Amarillo, Texas. Rows of wild bluebonnets grew with abandonment along the paved roadways, which spread out like a spider's web along the outskirts of the active runway. As we began our turn into the terminal, a military jeep with a large yellow "follow me" sign cut in ahead of us. There were no jetways designed for the massive airplane yet.

As we parked, two sets of air stairs were towed towards our aircraft. I had been offered the chance to ride in the cockpit as it was a ferry flight from JFK to Amarillo, and as I stood from my seat, a tall, uniformed man entered the cockpit. He saluted the crew and they reciprocated.

"Good morning, sir. Welcome to Amarillo. I am Airman Colletti, and I will be your liaison while you are here at our facility."

"Thank you, airman. I'm Captain Bonaventure, and this is my First Officer Sam Smithson, and my engineer, John Switzer. We've brought two of our mechanics along just in case. We don't want to burden the Air Force with any repairs that may come up."

"Thank you, sir."

"This is one long runway. Have you ever had a 747 land here before?"

First Officer Smithson asked.

"No, sir, you are the first. Pretty exciting, I gotta say." He smiled. "This runway was built for the USAF Strategic Air Command base. It's 13,502 feet long and among the longest commercial runways in the United States. We do a lot of training on it."

As he backed out of the cockpit he said, "If you need anything, please let us know. As soon as you depart for your hotel, we will be providing a twenty-four-hour watch on your airplane." He saluted again and left.

The senior agent, Melanie, stood at the door speaking quietly with a well-dressed older man, who handed her a packet – this normally contained information on the food service with details on any special passenger needs.

The crew gathered at the front of the plane as the man spoke. "You are flying some very rich and powerful men to Washington for a conference with the president. They're all connected to oil and gas in one way or another here in Texas – have you folks ever heard of T. Boone Pickens?"

The captain nodded but kept quiet.

"Well, he's the man footing the bill for this trip to Washington. He's a home-grown legend here in Amarillo. Sort of a 'pull-up by the boot-strap' kind of guy – and make a billion dollars while you're at it.' He laughed. "Not many can go from delivering newspapers to becoming a successful wildcatter here in Texas."

"Wildcatter? What's that?" one of the women asked.

"They drill for oil in fields not known to have oil. They take chances and hope for the best. Because he studied geology at Oklahoma State, he understands how to find oil."

"He sounds amazing," the woman said.

"Well, we're proud of him. He's sort of put us on the map." He cleared his throat. "Now, there should be about 250 businessmen including some wives. The flight will be catered for an abbreviated first class. I think it's steak and baked potatoes including a salad and cake for dessert. Plus of course, special champagne and cocktails – they're expecting the best."

He smiled as he turned to leave.

"Captain, what's the story on this T. Boone Pickens guy?" Melanie asked.

"Well, he's an impressive businessman. He's made his money in oil and gas explorations, according to *Forbes*. He is big into philanthropy, I think. I guess we'll find out more about him tomorrow."

We met the van driver, who was wearing a rather large cowboy hat and one of the biggest belt buckles I'd ever seen. He noticed the stares from my crew as they passed by him.

Pointing at the buckle he said, "I used to be a rodeo king. In my day, I rode some of the best broncos and meanest bulls in the state of Texas" he explained. "I earned this buckle fair and square. I'm proud of it."

As we were seated on the van, someone said, "Not much going on here – where are all the other airlines?"

"Well, most have already departed for the day," the driver said. "Braniff and Continental have one early flight a day, and Southwest doesn't fly here yet. And of course, there's the old TT Airlines, which is now Texas International."

"TT Airlines?"

"Trans Texas, was better known as Tree Top Airlines." The driver laughed as he smiled back at us. "They are a little-bitty airline with a big attitude. They only fly in Texas. They used to fly props, but now they fly DC-9's."

"Sounds like you have an axe to grind with them," the captain said.

"Nah, I just get tired of their obnoxious crews. I mean look at you guys, you're flying the biggest plane in the world and on top of that you're from New York City. You are way nicer than the crews of TT. I think they're trying to prove something."

"Maybe they're offended by the moniker Tree Top?" the captain offered.

The driver shrugged. "Maybe. In the early days, they gained that name by flying so close to the ground, I guess. Wow, look at this! Your arrival seems to have awakened this sleepy little town. It's normally very quiet at this time of day."

As he spoke, a local news crew was just pulling up to the gate. Three soldiers stopped them, their weapons at the ready.

"I'm glad to see that," the captain said, referencing the military protection. "That's all we need is someone messing with our plane."

"Oh, I wouldn't worry, sir. It's a military installation, and those military police are very tough on unwanted visitors, I reckon."

Our hotel/motel wasn't very memorable. It occupied a lonely hill that faced the main road. Attempts at planting flowers had failed; marigolds wilted at the grass deficient entrance. A few rundown cars and several trucks were parked near the entrance. When we checked in, the poor counter agent seemed overwhelmed. There were over twenty of us arriving at the same time. The captain handed the agent our crew list, which seemed to have a calming effect.

"We have instant coffee in the room, and there is a local diner where I'm sure your van will drop you off in the morning," the agent said as the van driver nodded. "Most of our lodgers go to the Bluebonnet Bar for dinner – it's right down the main road. If you wish for a wakeup call, please let us know before 8:00 P.M. Welcome, everyone."

The rooms were tiny, the smallest I had ever slept in on a layover. There were no tubs in the very small, and the beds were so hard we joked about bouncing pennies off them. I removed the bed spread on mine and placed it on the floor – it had seen better days.

Later, I joined a few crew members for dinner. I was hoping for a big ole steak. The concept of barbeque was very different in Texas: your steak would arrive crispy and black with some pink in the middle, just the way my dad cooked them.

Texas bars aren't known for their hospitality when you first come in; it takes a while for them to get to know you. This bar was no exception, and we got 'eyeballed' by the local cowboys until a waitress appeared.

We were strangers dressed like "fancies". Not one pair of dirty boots or a cowboy hat among us. I am sure they smelled New York on us. I was very adept at 'talking Texan' – I was from Texas, after all. My brother refused to give up his Texas accent and channeling him was a favorite pastime. Some small talk with the waitress who gave us the 'all clear' and we were in.

T-bones steaks were served all the way round. The Western music, beloved by the pilots, blared over the radio as we attempted to talk. A couple of local cowboys stopped by. When they discovered we flew in the 747, they were enthralled. It was late when one of them offered us a ride back to our hotel.

The next day, the same van driver – with the same enormous belt buckle - took us to the breakfast restaurant close to the airport. It wasn't designed like a regular restaurant – long benches lined a large dining room, very much like beer halls in Germany. We sat anywhere there was an empty space.

I sat next to two ladies dressed in what I soon discovered was a Texas International uniform. They stopped mid-bite of their salsa-covered scrambled eggs as we took our seats and stared at us.

I spoke first. "Good morning."

"Hi y'all," one of them replied.

As I sat in between the two women, I continued to feel their stares.

We, as a crew, were accustomed to stares from the public.

It was obvious that we were a crew, but the lady next to me asked an obvious question. "Are y'all with an airline?" she asked.

"Yes, we are." I could have told her who we flew for, but I felt like playing with her.

She was also with an airline, but our styles were worlds apart. There she sat wearing what appeared to be a straw hat with multicolored balls hanging from the rim. A white short-sleeved shirt was accompanied by a blue bolero and what appeared to be a very short skirt. The final play was the leather cowboy boots that were ornately carved with flowers.

"Well, where are y'all from?" she asked as she dumped a voluminous amount of hot sauce – from a bottle that warned of its 'mucho caliente' status – onto her scrambled eggs.

"We're from New York."

"New York, as in New York City?" the other stewardess declared. "What are y'all doing in Amarillo?"

Before I could answer the other TT woman said "Your uniforms are hot-looking. Don't you sweat in that material? I don't think I'd like wearing that all day."

Our uniforms were designed by Dalton. They could be toasty, and I did occasionally sweat, but I certainly wasn't going to admit that to her.

Somewhat offended, I countered with, "Well, I'm not much into Mexican Carnival hats either."

"Oh, this is just a promotional uniform for our new flights to Mexico." The other woman laughed. "We don't always wear these hats. If we get them on, we leave them on until the flight. They really mess with the bouffant hairdo. So, you never answered my question – why are you all down here?"

"We're on a charter flight," I replied as I buttered my toast. "Who are you with? I don't recognize your uniform."

"Why, we're Texas International – we're the biggest airline in the state of Texas. We used to be Trans Texas, but we just changed our name to

Texas International.”

(A 1967 radio commercial introduced the name change. The Trans Texas ad boldly proclaimed: “We've become a big airline, even bigger than Texas.”)

“Wow, that's pretty amazing. Where do you fly?” It was getting fun now – she was so proud, with her chest pushed out so far that I hated to stop.

“Well, we fly everywhere, in Texas that is.” She was now putting three teaspoons of sugar into her coffee. It nearly made me feel ill, thinking of her poor liver. “Where do you fly?” she asked.

“Well, we're an international airline. We fly all over the world, but not that much in Texas. We leave that to Braniff, Continental, and American. And I guess Trans Texas.”

“Yes, we know them. I tried to get a job with Braniff, but they said I was too short, the other woman interrupted.

“How tall are you?” I continued.

“Well, I'm five-foot. They said I had to be at least five-foot-two.”

“We have that same regulation. Our overhead bins are so high on the 747, they're thinking of increasing that minimum height regulation.”

“What's a 747?” she asked.

“It's the newest wide-bodied airplane to be added to our fleet by Boeing.”

“Well, I bet our plane is bigger. We just got DC9s added to our fleet. We have nine now,” she boasted.

I didn't want to make her feel any worse by comparing sizes. Fortunately, the van driver appeared at the door. “Time to go, ladies and gentlemen,” he shouted with a wave of his hand.

As I stood, I said, “It was lovely meeting you.”

“We will probably see you at the airport, but if not, have a good flight,” she replied.

“Thanks, you too.”

As the van entered the gates of the airport, I saw the Texas International jet sitting near our 747. It seemed small, but then every airplane seemed small compared to the 747.

As I began to board the airstairs to our plane, the Texas International crew pulled in. I purposely took my time walking up the stairs until at the top, I turned to see the Texas International crew emerge from the van.

They stood in awe, eyes wide open and jaws ajar as they marveled at the size of the 747. She was indeed a spectacular sight.

I waved my hand to them and said, "Goodbye, biggest little airline in the state of Texas. Best of luck to you."

** TT Airlines became Texas International in 1969. However, after it suffered unrecoverable losses in 1982, It was absorbed by Continental Airlines and the 'Frank Lorenzo' group.

CHAPTER TWENTY-TWO

THAT SINKING FEELING

One day, I was on a call-out to Frankfurt with a stop in London. It was cold and windy outside, and I shivered as I walked down the hallway to the briefing room. The rooms never seemed to be heated, and today was no exception. Today's flight was on a Boeing 707, which unlike a 747, briefed at Hangar 12. On cold and windy days, the wind seemed to seep into the very seams of our small rooms; I always thought it might be because the hangar door stayed open to service broken planes.

We had already finished bidding for our work positions, and after discussing the new dinner menu, we waited for the appearance of the cockpit crew. They normally came, introduced themselves, and filled us in on potential weather problems and flight times. When it became obvious that they weren't coming, the purser stood, gathered his belongings, and we followed him to the terminal bus.

On the aircraft, the captain was seated in the cabin, speaking quietly to the engineer. We learned that the engineer was brand-new. This was his first actual trip. The first officer, filling in for the captain, briefed us as the gate agent announced boarding

We reached London around 6:00 P.M., and after our local passengers deplaned, each crewmember found a place to hide while cabin service cleaned the aircraft for the domestic run to Frankfurt. I seated myself in the last row of first class, close to the window.

Just before we began boarding, I walked to the galley and noticed from the open galley door a confrontation between the captain and the new engineer. The captain was clearly agitated, waving his arms and pointing at the airplane, and I heard the words, "walk around" and "oil and tires."

It seemed the engineer might have missed a step or two." Every engineer was assigned to walk around the entire airplane observing potential inflight hazards, a procedure intended to determine if there are any unknown issues with the landing gears, engines, or exterior parts of the airplane. I hoped the new guy had done his job today.

It was 7:00 in the evening by the time the plane took off from Heathrow Airport, on its way to Germany. The flight would be a short ninety minutes, and the mood of the passengers was quiet. Most, if not all, were European. Only a dead-heading TWA crew were seated in First Class – disinterested in food or drinks, they immediately hunkered down with pillows and blankets for a short nap.

A soft drink service was scheduled in coach, and I concentrated on arranging my serving tray with choices of Coke, 7-Up, and an occasional ginger ale – water with a lemon slice was also helpful to identify it at night. As I reached for my fully loaded tray of drinks, I felt a slight dip, and it felt like the galley was lowering ever so slightly under my tray. I glanced at my partner, Loretta, who was fully engrossed in preparing another tray for me. She was oblivious.

I felt unsteady as I tried walking down the aisle of the Boeing 707, the plane once again moving downward. I had to adjust the tray quickly so that it did not hit the top of a passenger's seat.

Most of the reading lights were off, and very few passengers seemed interested in the beverage service. Just as I looked down the aisle to see if anyone else had felt the downward slip, the cabin lights dimmed and the emergency lights flickered on. The emergency lights were designed to replace cabin lights, in the event that power ceased to be supplied by the engines, and in a second, they flickered off and the cabin lights re-lit.

What? Did I really see that? I thought.

As I puzzled over this, a man asked for a Coke. It was then that I realized that I had nearly lost all the drinks. They had started sliding precariously toward the edge of the tray.

I looked down the aisle, and once again I saw the emergency lights flicker this time combined with the changing of engine pitch. I could have sworn that the engines were "spooling down," a term used for when engines begin to wind down.

Perhaps it is just my imagination? "What the hell is going on?" I said out loud, though quietly enough that only I could hear.

Taking a good look around the cabin, I could tell that the passengers did not share my curiosity. The ones who were awake were reading, totally immersed in their own worlds.

Turning on my heel, I returned to the galley.

"Did you see that?" I asked Loretta, who was busily pouring soft drinks.

"See what?" She stopped and stared at me. "Are you okay? You're white as a sheet."

The engines were sounding strong and normal, and, staring back into the cabin, I began to wonder how to explain my thoughts. Suddenly, the emergency lights came on again – this time, however, they stayed on. Now the few passengers who were awake were looking around, though still not unduly alarmed.

Our altitude dropped precipitously. "That!" I said to Loretta, who was now on her knees picking up items that had tumbled to the floor.

"Go," she breathed quietly. I knew she meant to go to the cockpit, and I quickly walked up there. When I approached the front, Lydia, the senior hostess, looked up at me with a curious stare.

"Something wrong?" she said, reading the anxiety in my face.

"I don't know – did you feel the plane drop? The emergency lights went on back there."

"No, we didn't feel anything," she replied. All the First-Class lights were turned off so the dead headers could sleep, and the emergency lights above the doors were not visible in the cabin, blocked on one side by a partition and on the other by the galley.

"I'm going to find out what's going on." I said, bravely walking towards the cockpit.

I knocked twice and waited for the door to be opened, but there was no response. I knocked again, and after what seemed like an eternity, the engineer opened the door. As I grabbed the doorknob, I was brought to my knees by another drop of the plane. Sounds of unsecured items crashing to the galley floor resounded.

The emergency lights in the cockpit glowed. Both pilots were so immersed in their tasks that my presence was not noted. The flight engineer returned to flipping switches and the captain was barking a cockpit checklist along with the first officer. I knew they were in no mood to chit chat with me, so I quietly closed the door.

The other hostesses, including Loretta, were all now standing in the galley with Lydia. As I closed the door, Lydia asked, "Well, what did they say?"

"Nothing," I said. "They were all flipping buttons and yelling out checklists. I didn't think it was the time to interrupt them."

"What do you think is happening?" one of the hostesses said.

"Who knows?" Lydia said. "Let's just get the cabin prepared, just in case."

"Just in case?" I asked.

"Of an emergency." Loretta said.

"Yes," Lydia confirmed.

"Are the passengers aware?" another hostess asked.

"I think we're okay for now, but we need some communication from the front," Lydia said, her face serious. "Secure your galleys; prepare for an emergency landing. Do not say a word to the passengers – we'll wait for the captain. I'll go up there when we get ready. Go!"

We all walked quickly through the cabin collecting items, relieved that we had only been serving drinks and not a full dinner service.

Soon, with all cabin items and galleys secured and stowed, we were now ready for an emergency landing, aside from telling the passengers. As we waited for communication from the front, the emergence of the cabin lights signaled that we were back in business.

Moments later, Lydia called and announced that we were beginning descent. "Prepare for a normal landing, not an emergency," she said.

"How much longer before we land?" I asked.

"About fifteen minutes."

I sat in my jump seat, trying to recall all that had just happened. I knew that if someone wrote us up, either a passenger or crew, I'd have to write a report; we all would.

After a normal landing, the passengers deplaned, and we headed for customs. As we walked to our crew bus, the cockpit crew purposely ignored us, and as the crew bus drove carefully through the darken streets of Mainz, Germany, the normal joviality of the crew was missing.

At the hotel, the captain signed us in and announced that dinner would be at the Hofbrau Church at 9:00 P.M. as previously planned. Then all three pilots left, without a word. Expecting at least an explanation as to what occurred during the flight, we were all somewhat miffed.

Lydia spoke softly: "Okay, let's get dressed. We'll get some answers at dinner. Be down here in thirty." I had a feeling that tonight she would shine.

The hotel rooms in Germany were large and sweet-smelling, and I loved the perfumed bath salts that awaited me as I laid out my outfit. I ran a very hot bath in the enormous tub, wishing I had time to really soak – thirty minutes wasn't long enough to wash off 16 hours of sweat and cigarette smoke. This dinner was an important fact-finding mission, however, so I rushed my bath and dressed hastily.

Meeting downstairs, one of the women reported the captain had already left to secure us a table. The restaurant, a very popular eating establishment, was well attended by other airline crews, so tables would be difficult to find, especially for seven people.

Raucous revelers, singing in German, pushed past us on the narrow, cobbled streets.

This restaurant was exceptional and located a short four blocks from our hotel, it was in a partially bombed out church, which had been ingeniously renovated around the blackened beams. Photos of Germany on the wall, prior to and following the war, brought the war alive for the many pilots who fought in it. Intense conversations were often heard over the loud requests for "a pint."

When we arrived at the restaurant, our crew was thankfully already seated. Hunger pangs reminded me that I had not eaten since New York, many hours earlier.

Wine and beer were ordered, and the waiters handed us all menus. I never looked at a menu in Germany because I knew what I wanted: *swinehocken mit saurerkrauts* – pork hocks cooked in sauerkraut. This meal always made my partners cringe – something about a pork knuckle covered in smelly sauerkraut was abhorrent to my crew.

The captain had turned to another table, speaking intently to another pilot. Our first officer and flight engineer were listening closely, and I thought that they were probably rehashing the curious events during our flight.

I watched as Lydia stared at the captain's head, waiting for her turn to speak. She never got her chance – he suddenly pushed his chair out abruptly and rose to leave, excusing himself. His conversation with the other man had been loud, although the words were indiscernible, and we wondered if something was going to happen as the two men walked out of the restaurant.

The first officer moved from across the table and sat down next to Lydia. The two of them, both married, had been having a torrid affair for years, and it was known that they met and consummated their relationship overseas. He touched her hand and said something to her gently, but she was not in the mood. She said something that caused him to pull away and shake his head in a slow, decisive manner.

Damn, this is one weird crew. At this point, I wished I was in Rome. I would at least have been intoxicated and pinched by at least three Italians by now. The other women, meanwhile, were conversing about their children, which I did not find the least bit interesting.

Out of nowhere, the captain came back, all red-faced like he had been in a verbal fight. He sat down across the table from Lydia, who was now silent and pensive. Not saying a word, he grasped a half-filled beer mug and swallowed the entire contents of it.

In a seething rage, Lydia reached across the table, grabbing him by the tie and pulling him halfway across the table in one fell swoop and meeting him the rest of the way with her body. Face to face, they stood over the beer mugs and candles, her hand still firmly around his tie.

"Okay, Jess," she said, in a spitting fury, "what the hell happened up there tonight?"

As his hand reached over hers to loosen her grip, the two of them slowly sat down in their seats.

After composing himself he said, not very convincingly, "What are you talking about?"

"Oh please – give us a little credit for paying attention." She was indignant.

A sheepish grin spread over his face. "Well, we supposed that because you never came running and screaming into the cockpit, you didn't notice anything."

"Didn't notice the plane losing altitude, or the cabin lights dimming while the engines spooled down? Yeah, that's easy to overlook!" She was in a fit now.

We all waited as the captain sat in silence. The first officer and flight engineer both stared sheepishly at the table.

"Ladies," the captain said, "some things are on a need-to-know basis, and I think this is one of them." Smiling at all of us, he became quiet.

I thought that was probably a true statement, since I was totally ignorant of anything to do with jet engines, and the less I knew the better. Especially at 36,000 feet over the Atlantic – that's when I really didn't want to know anything, as there was absolutely nothing, I could do to change my situation.

Incredulously Lydia spoke with a total air of insubordination when she said, "Cut the crap. Unless you want us to share this 'little incident' with the company, you better speak up, buddy."

The scene was intense – I had never in my short career witnessed a captain being dressed down by a hostess.

The other customers were fortunately either speaking German or unable to decipher what was being said over the din of conversation and accordion music.

"Well?" she said. "What happened? I want to know! We all have a right to know, and it's not privileged information since we were all involved!"

With a look that could have killed, he again took a moment to compose his thoughts. Looking at the other two pilots – who were managing to look at their laps, he finally spoke. "It seems that someone accidentally flipped a breaker."

"Someone?" She looked straight at the flight engineer.

"Yes, someone." The captain met her glance.

During this moment, the flight engineer had found something very interesting in the lining of his coat and had decided to investigate it.

"Well, can you explain to me what the consequences of this little mistake could have been?" Lydia knew the answer, but she clearly wanted to take this all the way.

His eyes blazed. "It could have been very ugly. Is that what you want to hear?" he shouted.

"No, not really – that's not at all what I wanted to hear! I wanted to hear that you guys have your shit together. I wanted to hear that our lives are safe up there. I didn't want to hear that someone accidentally flipped a breaker."

She rose from the table. "Where are you going?" the captain asked.

"I am going to check my underwear – I think I just crapped in my pants!" she said.

The table was silent for a moment, until an old friend of the captain approached the table and the conversation restarted.

Did I ever find out what *really* happened up there that night? The answer is no. Just like many mysterious things that happen on an airplane, I will never know. In a quest for an answer, I have asked seasoned retired pilots and mechanics, and I've researched the workings of Boeing 707s. I do not want to distort the safety record of TWA in any way, but what I've found is that, in error, the very junior flight engineer must have either flipped the fuel supply switch or the generator bus switch – either one could have caused this incident. In my long career at TWA, there was never a time before or after this incident when I felt unsafe, and in many ways, I am thankful that this incident remains a mystery.

CHAPTER TWENTY-THREE

PALMA DE MAJORCA, JANUARY 1972

New York City has never been known for having pleasant weather in January, and this year was no exception. I was now living in Long Island, where the ocean kept the snow at bay – in exchange, however, we endured high winds that whipped the ocean's waves into a white foam.

I enjoyed walking on the beach in the aftermath of a storm, comparing its stark beauty with my memories of Redondo Beach and its peaceful ocean. But today, after receiving a phone call from the crew scheduler, I was feeling thrilled about my upcoming assignment to Palma de Majorca, Spain.

I started packing immediately, my swimsuit being the first item in my bag. I had little to no information about the city, but I knew anything would be better than 35 degrees.

I met my crew at the JFK terminal, where I soon learned we were being sent to rescue a charter group waiting to return to the states; their scheduled flight crew was stuck in Canada. The Toronto bound airplane had slid off an icy runway, incurring minor damage. The crew were ordered to stay with the plane and ferry it back to New York when repairs were finished – I could only imagine how angry they were to discover that we were replacing them. Our crew would be dead-heading to Madrid on a TWA 747, and then Iberia Airlines would take us from Madrid to Palma de Majorca.

Our flight to Madrid was fortunately spent in First Class, where I was treated to a smorgasbord of both delightful music and delicious food. As we approached Madrid, the plane ride became bumpy, and the captain explained that a storm was passing through the airspace.

When we arrived in Madrid, the weather was getting even nastier, with occasional downpours and plenty of thunder. Surprisingly, as we boarded the Iberia airplane, we noticed a rather relaxed and cheerful attitude among the Iberian crew – they seemed unaware of, or complacent about, the impending storm, even as lightning flashed continuously.

The crew barely noticed us as we marched by the open cockpit door; not a "howdy" or "how are you doing?" left their lips, and the stewardesses were busy gossiping in the galley.

Our captain followed airline protocol, stowing his luggage and then proceeding to the cockpit to make introductions. When he returned, he whispered to the First Officer that he detected a strong smell of alcohol in the cockpit. This was not unheard of in our occupation, but it made us feel uneasy, since the weather was getting worse.

As the plane left the gate, the joviality continued. The Iberia captain made announcements with the cockpit door wide open – which was a "no-no" in our world – and it stayed open for takeoff and during most of the flight.

All his announcements were in Spanish, and they caused some of the passengers to laugh, others to look at us as they giggled. The stewardesses also continued the comedy when it came time to give their announcements.

Our purser, fluent in Spanish, soon translated the comments. "They're clearly making fun of us – well, actually you," she said, speaking to our captain. "The Iberian captain said he's going to show the Americans how well the Spanish can fly a plane."

"Well, that's not surprising to hear," the captain said quietly. "I think he's intoxicated. Let's see how funny he is when he must fly through the thunderstorms that are building all around us. Well, I guess if we have to help him out, he's made it easier to do so – the cockpit door is wide open."

The First Officer turned and whispered to us: "Buckle up, ladies. It's going to be a bumpy ride."

And that it was. When the plane dropped precipitously, one Iberia stewardess, tempting fate, hit the ceiling hard. As the once-funny girl crawled down the aisle to her jumpseat, our purser offered to help her.

From then on, the joviality ceased – the Iberia crew no longer had the cockpit door open and their girls stayed in their seats.

The landing at the Palma de Mallorca Airport was safe, thankfully, although not as smooth as we were accustomed to. As we deplaned, we heard a female Iberia crew member heaving in the forward lavatory, a reminder not to "drink and fly."

As our luggage was being loaded in our van, we noticed the Iberia crew being pelted by a fresh rainstorm as they struggled to help a female crew member get into their van, their uniforms soaked.

As we watched, I heard the captain say, "Karma."

The van eventually arrived at our destination, the Hotel Victoria, which is located on the Bay of Palma. Even in the rainy darkness, I could see how the hotel, built in 1912, must have once been a grand fixture in this city. The driver explained that it had once served as the premiere spot for the locals and tourists to wine and dine.

Oversized doors opened into a large atrium, with a wide sweeping stairway on one side and an elaborate counter on the other. Baroque sculptures towered over multiple ornate water fountains situated throughout. The restaurant, which was now closed, was to the left of the stairway. As I peeked in, I could barely see the darkened harbor through the large, plate glass windows –a few small boats were moored, their flags fluttered in the rain.

No one in the TWA crew had visited Palma, so there wasn't a plan for our unusually long layover. We were hungry – eight hours had passed since our last meal – but sleep was now our priority. We all agreed we would plan the next day's activities at breakfast and after a good night's rest. The girls and I wandered up to our rooms, leaving the pilots to discuss having a drink at the bar.

My room was especially spacious, with large velvet drapes that covered towering windows facing the harbor. I tried opening a window to get some fresh air, but I discovered it had been painted shut.

After a hot bath, I was lulled into a blissful sleep, dreaming of balmy weather and sunshine.

Early the next day, the storm had passed, and the warm rays of the sun awakened me. As usual, it took a moment to remind myself of where I was. Normally on layovers, a crew call from Paris announced where you were and the time, and they reminded you of the departure time of the airport bus. With no flight to catch, and no crew call, this really did feel like a vacation – I could get used to these 48-hour layovers.

As I made my way down to the restaurant, I could hear voices, mostly male. At the bottom of the staircase, I could see through the restaurant window – in the distance, there appeared to be an aircraft carrier.

As I turned to make my entrance into the dining room, I was surprised to see that the entire room was filled with men, all dressed in white – Navy whites. It took me a minute but then it hit me – the men in white? Well, they were officers of the U.S. Navy.

Of course, I had to make a grand entrance, so when I walked into the room, I asked, "Whose big boat is that?"

A man stood, and as he did, everyone else followed suit. The man, whom I was sure might topple over from all the metals pinned to his chest, approached me and asked, "Would you like to join us for breakfast, Miss?"

I laughed. "All of you?" The men all laughed. "Why yes, I'd love that."

I followed him to a table. "Who are you all?" I asked.

"We are Attack Squadron 87, well known as 'The Golden Warriors.' My name is Commander Jack Fetterman, and these men are stationed on that 'big boat' out there. It is the U.S.S. Roosevelt."

"Wow, that's a mouthful," I giggled. I took his hand and sat down. A loud scraping of chairs followed as the men also sat.

The waitress appeared and as I ordered, he began to ask questions: "Now, who are you, Miss? And what are *you* doing here?"

"Well, my name is Dianna. I work for TWA. My crew and I are working a charter to New York on Wednesday. I'm sorry I called your ship a boat; I hope I didn't offend the U.S. Navy."

The commander smiled as he said, "The U.S. Navy is not easily offended."

A few moments later, my girls showed up and found themselves also sitting with the other officers for breakfast.

Commander Fetterman explained that the ship was in port until Sunday "If you all are interested, you are invited to visit the carrier. We have 6,000 men assigned to the Roosevelt whom I am sure would love to show you ladies around their home."

"I'd love to, but I can't speak for the others," I said. "Let me see what the other girls want to do."

He nodded and pointed to the back of the hotel. "In order to get to our ship, you will take a 'tender,'" he said. "They are smaller boats located right down there, and they leave every hour to and from our ship. I will inform the officer of the deck to be on the lookout for you five lovely ladies."

With that, Commander Fetterman stood, as did all his men. As they filed out of the restaurant, I joined my crew. "Well, what do you guys want to do?" I asked.

One of the girls leaned forward, "I thought there were beaches here, but I asked, and the concierge said that the beaches are about twenty minutes away. It's not cheap getting there, either."

"The crew said last night that they'd meet us down here at 10 A.M. – they wanted to sleep in after going to the bar. I guess it was a late night," another added.

"Well, I don't know about you guys," I said. "But I'm accepting the invitation. It's not often you get a personal invitation from a Navy commander to see an aircraft carrier."

"And all those *men*," one girl whispered.

"Let's leave a note for the pilots," another said.

"Let's not," I said. "They didn't invite us out last night."

The tender swiftly transported us to the carrier, along with several other tourists.

"Well ladies, this is one for the record books," one of the women shouted above the drone of the boat.

"Yes," I said, "when you're asked what you did on your layover, you can just say, 'Well I walked around an aircraft carrier with 6,000 men, how about you?'" We all laughed.

The ship was immense. We were whistled on board by the 'officer of the deck'. I'd seen that in the movies, and I must admit, that felt special.

Each of the girls departed on their personal tour, each escorted by two officers, one on either side of them. My escort turned out to be Commander Fetterman – it was flattering to be given so much attention by one with such power.

"So, Commander –" I said.

He interrupted me: "Jack, that's my name. Commander is my title." He smiled.

"Okay," I said, "so where are you all headed?"

"We are on a Mediterranean cruise. We are just here as a show of force."

Walking down the deck, we approached a group of men, and I watched as everyone readily saluted him. I thought how exhausting it all must be, responding to the salutes. "So, Jack, what made you decide to join the Navy?"

"I joined because I had dreamed of flying ever since I was a little boy. I scoured the libraries growing up, reading about famous pilots, from 'Lucky Lindy' to Chuck Yeager. I just wanted to fly. As soon as I graduated from college, I joined the Navy." He laughed. "And here I am."

"How long have you been a Navy man?" I asked.

"Let's see. I applied at Naval Air Station Pensacola in 1955, so seventeen years. Is anyone in your family in the military?"

"Yes, my father was in the Army. He's recently retired." I replied.

"Any military action?"

"Nope, not really. He served in the Aleutian Islands, where his unit killed a Kodiak bear."

"Well, that's interesting – tell me about it."

"Really? Okay, well it seems this bear attacked their encampment while they slept – the guard had apparently fallen asleep, and several men were injured. One died of his injuries; I believe."

"Wow, the guard was sleeping – that's unbelievable."

I laughed. "Lesson learned? Never zip your sleeping bag all the way up."

"Why?"

"Because" I said, "if it gets stuck and you panic, you can succumb to a bear attack."

He laughed a good belly laugh. It made me happy to laugh with him; it made him seem human.

We spent the day walking the ship, which I learned was lovingly called "Rosie" by some of the men. I was also treated to lunch in the Officers' Wardroom. I can't recall what we had to eat – I was too nervous to be around so many men in such a small room. I wondered if my girls were eating with their adoring hosts; I hadn't spotted them all day.

After lunch, we surprised a few of the unsuspecting men as we walked through their bedrooms. I also rode up and down on the lifts designed to move the aircraft from each deck, and lastly, we visited the Pri-Fly, which translates to the Primary Flight Control. I saw his squadron of A-7 Corsairs lined up on the deck and I could tell that my new friend Jack was proud to call them his "Warriors."

As dusk approached, I managed to gather the girls together, and we made our goodbyes. We were given Golden Warriors stickers and a few hugs. Commander Fetterman and I exchanged addresses, although I doubted, I'd ever hear from him.

As we left the ship, our hearts swelled with pride, knowing all these young men were there to protect our democracy.

The next day as we met downstairs to drive to the airport, the tension was palpable – the pilots seemed angry. It was understandable; they hadn't seen or heard from us for twenty-four hours.

"We looked for you ladies everywhere. It was only when I was given the message that you were visiting the U.S.S Roosevelt that we were clear where you were." The captain was spitting his words as he spoke.

"I didn't realize we had to check in with you guys?" I said.

"We said we'd meet at 10 to make a plan."

"Well, we made our own plans," I said. "We were given a chance to see an aircraft carrier, so we took it. We knew you guys weren't interested in going." They were Army and Marine pilots, after all.

One of the women later confessed that she had left a note telling the captain that we were visiting the ship. The tension was exacerbated when they spotted the Navy Golden Warriors stickers on our otherwise pristine white crew kits.

Commander Fetterman did indeed write to me. I responded to his letters several times, until I realized that he was seventeen years my senior. I expressed that perhaps we should remain friends, and then I never heard from him again. He was a kind and ethical man whom I was privileged to meet. We, as a nation, were lucky to have him in our military, as history will prove.

CHAPTER TWENTY-FOUR

STAR WITNESS CONCLUDES, 1978

So much can happen in six years.

In 1972, after I made my statement to the Jersey City police, they convinced TWA that living in New York City wasn't healthy for me. The brothers had killed once and were currently free, awaiting their trial for murder – what if they happened to meet up with me on the mean streets of New York?

When asked where I'd like to live, I chose Kansas City. I was in a serious relationship with a man who lived there, and the timing was right, so I requested a transfer.

Upon arrival in Kansas City, my measly two years of seniority did not go unnoticed by the senior hostesses. How did I, a newbie, come by a coveted bid to their very senior base? The rumors swirled – did I pay someone off? Was I sent there to spy on their performance? Or was I a protected witness? The truth remained buried in a file that was only accessible by a court order.

So, when 1978 rolled around, I was living in obscurity, I thought, with my new husband. We had a lovely house on a parcel of land in Stilwell, Kansas, not far from the Kansas City International Airport. We were married in 1976, and I gave birth to a little girl named Anne Marie in 1977. In short order, I had managed to melt into the Kansas City flying community. The rumors had died down and I was now flying domestic routes weekly. In the excitement that came from my new life, the homicide case and subsequent trial had been all but forgotten.

One sunny spring day in late May, two men arrived at my doorstep. They were met by my very large and very unsociable German Shepard, her low growl assuring me that these two men had bad intentions. As I approached the door, I recognized Detective O'Leary and Detective Petroski, realizing instantly that my past life had come to visit.

"Well, you picked a good protector there." Detective O'Leary said, raising his hands.

Detective Petroski smiled. "Yes, there's no sneaking up on her."

"Hey detectives," I said. "Welcome to my home. I hope you're not bringing bad news." I smiled as I held onto the collar of my dog. "Let's go inside – she's calmer now, and she only bites if I tell her to." I giggled.

After settling in and offering the two men some lemonade, they shared their reasons for visiting me.

"First, I want to say, you are one difficult woman to find," Detective O'Leary said.

"Yes – we've been trying to locate you for over three months. Your company meant it when they said they'd seal your file," Detective Petroski said. "It seems they lost your file. We had to get a court order to find you."

"I'm sorry," I said, very unconvincingly.

"So you're married? Detective Petroski asked.

"Yes. He's from New York. He transferred here and I followed."

"And your new name is Bennett now?" he continued.

"Yes."

Detective O'Leary looked out of the large picture window and swept his hand around. "This is quite a transition from your New York life. I mean, there's cows walking around out there."

"Yes, we have cows and horses and chickens and ducks." I laughed. "I'll take you for a tour if you have time."

He shook his head. "I'm afraid we need to get right back, so down to business. The trial starts in one week at the courthouse, and the court is summoning you to return and testify."

I could feel my blood pressure rise as I contemplated a return to New York. I would be leaving the safety of my home, my young daughter, and the security of my husband. I knew I had no choice but to comply, but I now regretted ever having recognized Ronnie Chaney.

I laughed a weak laugh. "I'm impressed that you both came all the way out here. We have mail too, you know?"

Detective Petroski smiled. "The prosecutor wanted us to visually confirm that it was indeed you, plus he wanted confirmation that you were coming to the trial next week. Your eyewitness account is the key to putting these two killers in jail."

He handed me a large Manila envelope and continued: "You can read this information later – it contains an overview of the trial, and your airline tickets. They aren't in first class; I hope you don't mind."

Detective O'Leary leaned forward. "There's also a court order that says you must hang out in Jersey City until you are called to the stand to testify. You will be on the city's dime, which is more like five cents." He laughed and continued: "Your hotel accommodations won't be what you're accustomed to, but we will do our best."

I laughed. "I'll probably use my company passes – save you money AND sit in First Class. Can I return home over the weekend? I have a baby girl, you know? I'm confident my husband won't allow her to come with me."

"As far as I know, if the trial continues over the weekend, and if the judge allows, you will be allowed to return home." Detective O'Leary said.

This was a relief to know I wouldn't be gone much longer than a long flight assignment. I had an excellent babysitter, but I still was concerned about a long absence from my baby girl.

I walked the two men to their car, fearing my dog's delayed retribution on them for arriving uninvited. They appeared relieved, knowing that one more piece to the unending puzzle of this murder was in place.

"We will see you next week." As they drove down my driveway they waved. And for the first time since I met them in 1972, I cried. The fear was becoming increasingly real.

One week later, I landed at Newark Airport, where O'Leary and Petroski were waiting for me at the gate. Their car, which had lights and sirens this time, was driven by a very official looking, uniformed officer. Clearly excited about the long-awaited prospect of placing the two men in prison for murder, the detectives chatted incessantly. I wasn't really listening – I was too busy wondering how I would manage this new and unreal world of murder. *How did I find myself here? What if I had just lied about seeing the twin? It would have been so easy.* But I was young and free then, without a care in the world. Not like today, where I was burdened with thoughts of my family.

We arrived at the courthouse, where I was to meet with the prosecutor who would try the brothers.

When I entered the room, the prosecutor stood. He was an older, balding man in an ill-fitting suit. It was not a look that inspired confidence, but who was I to judge?

"Well, it's good to finally meet you, Miss – we certainly appreciate your cooperation. I hope this will be a speedy trial so we can return you to your home – and your little girl, is it?" The prosecutor reached to shake my hand.

"Yes, thank you," I said as I sat in the chair that he had pulled out for me.

Once I was sitting, the prosecutor launched right into things: "This trial has been going on since January, and we have exhausted all our efforts in trying to locate you, fearful that our 'ace in the hole' was lost. You will be required to attend court each day – we don't know when you will be called to the stand. You will be seated outside the courtroom, and I must inform you that the Chaney family and friends will most likely be there in force. We have assigned an officer to accompany you for added protection."

"Added protection?" I asked.

"The family is very large, and so far, they've been quite verbal, though not physical, in their attacks on our case. They feel that Johnnie Chaney is being wrongfully tried; they've all bought up this scenario about him being in San Francisco, far away from the murder scene. There are witnesses who are attempting to corroborate Ronnie Chaney's false story about being at a friend's house rather than on your flight, and you are the only one to unravel his lie. So, you will never be left alone. Better safe than sorry." He smiled unconvincingly.

I'm a so-called protected witness, yet I must sit near antagonists who want to hurt me. I had yet to see where I would be sitting each day, but anywhere close to them was too close for me. "Why can't I sit in the courtroom with everyone else?" I whined.

"It's not allowed. You are a witness; it's the law."

Tentacles of fear began creeping into my mind. I was so far away from home, and motherhood had changed my courageous heart. My little girl was well cared for, but what of *my* well being? I hadn't considered that by testifying my life might be in jeopardy.

Detective Petroski broke the silence. "Let's get you checked in and then get you some lunch."

We all stood and the prosecutor returned to his work, oblivious of the mounting fear that his words had created. I wasn't confident anymore *– did I really see the twin on my flight?*

As if he had read my mind, Detective O'Leary said, "Let's all take a little walk downstairs to the jail to remind you of what good old Ronnie looks like now."

Before I could argue, I found myself staring at the man I had picked out of a group of photos, six years earlier. As I stared at him through a one-way mirror, I knew he was probably unaware that I was the one person who might imprison him and his brother.

As we left the jail, Detective Petroski said, "Are you okay?

I nodded. "Yes, I'm fine; I'm just a little shaken. I guess I never imagined all of this. Are you sure that I will be safe?"

"Dianna, we have protected State's witnesses many times. We will be right next to your room at night. Unfortunately, we can't take you out to dinner, but we will deliver anything your heart desires." Detective O'Leary touched my shoulder as he spoke. I felt somewhat better, but honestly, I understood now why people refused to engage in the eyewitness process.

My hotel was one step up from my first apartment in New York – the bed wasn't too lumpy, but the linens were questionable. I removed the bedspread, which I would never sit on, anyway – you never know what's been on them. Otherwise, the room was clean, and the towels were ample. As I unpacked my clothing, I hoped I had enough clothes for a week.

Each new day, the detectives met me at my door, coffee and rolls in hand. The nights were filled with strange sounds outside my room, but I knew a police officer was hopefully awake, listening for my screams.

I spent each day seated on a hard bench, waiting to hear my name echoing down the hall. Members of the opposing family sat on the other side of the hall, staring at me – hard – and occasionally making loud comments to try to unnerve me. My protector, a uniformed police officer, occasionally demanded that they "pipe down."

Lunch was eaten daily in the prosecutor's office, where I was privy to insider discussions and updates on the case. I soon realized how carefully the brothers had planned their murder, planting multiple witnesses to corroborate their movements before, during, and after the murder. The name on the airline ticket was "Mr. Chaney," so therefore either brother could have flown – it was ingenious.

There was an actual witness to the shooting, but her testimony became tainted by changes in the facts she gave during both her *voir dire* and the actual trial. I honestly think she was afraid to tell the truth – the brothers were ruthless. I soon came to understand why my facial recognition was key to the case.

I must say I did enjoy sending the detectives in search of my cravings for dinner. There were Chinese nights and Italian nights, and often I'd tell them to surprise me.

On Friday night, I flew home to see my husband and child, sworn to secrecy about the case. On Sunday evening I returned to my small motel room.

The day finally arrived when the bailiff shouted my name. I jumped, as did my protector. We had been ensconced in a crossword puzzle – in the two weeks that I sat in the hall, I had become friends with a few of the young police officers who sat next to me, and I had come to believe that they would take a bullet for me, or at least I hoped they would.

The courtroom was eerily quiet when I walked in, and a few people turned to watch me take the stand. I heard someone say, "Lying Bitch!" The judge demanded they be removed from his courtroom.

The defense pounced on me as soon as I finished taking the oath: "So, Ms. Shockley, how had you come to recognize Mr. Ronnie Chaney on the airplane?" The judge had agreed that my new name would not be used, in an effort to continue my anonymity.

Understanding the inference, the prosecutor interrupted with, "She didn't know anything about the murder when she identified Ronnie Chaney. She just recalled his face and his unusual actions on her flight."

Then the defense asked if there were any black flight attendants on the flight. My mind swirled as I tried to recall the cabin crew from that day. We had so few black flight hostesses that I was sure I would have recalled if one had worked with me, and the ones who flew out of New York were easily qualified to be beauty queens and highly memorable.

My brother-in-law, an attorney in New York, had coached me on what to say. He had said that one can never be absolutely sure of anything, therefore you should always say "to the best of my recollection." He promised it would slow down the defense's attacks.

"Were there any other black men on your flight on this day in question?" the defense questioned.

"Not to my knowledge," I replied.

"Then how come you remember Ronnie Chaney, as you've testified?" He was shouting now.

After a caution from the judge, I was asked to finish answering the question. "The only reason I remember Ronnie Chaney was because I was drawn to his unusual actions – so much so that I took notes, just in case he wrote a bad letter." I replied.

"Unusual actions? Can you explain further?" a quieter, chastised defense attorney asked.

"He seemed afraid or unsure of himself. I can't explain how I knew, but I felt like he didn't want to be on my plane. Most of our passengers are relaxed and excited – his body language and actions were unusual. He refrained from food and a free movie, sat in a middle seat, and never left that seat in the seven hours of flight."

"Did you notice him because he was black?" The defense attorney was shouting again. He clearly thought he was on to something, and I could sense that he was trying to wind me up and get me to say something stupid.

The judge again cautioned him. "Go ahead, Ms. Shockley. Was the color of his skin a factor in your memory?"

I answered defiantly. "We are trained to treat all races equally. I didn't write 'black male' in my notes on my flight log. It wasn't a factor."

"I rest, your honor." The defense attorney sat.

The prosecutor then read my original statement from 1972, which helped to clarify my comments.

There was a lot of back and forth by the defense in an attempt to undermine my testimony.

When they finally rested, the prosecutor rose and began walking me through my involvement with the case. The moment finally came when he told me to stand and point out the man who was on my flight that fateful day, I stood and pointed to Ronnie Chaney and said, "To the best of my recollection, that is the man who was on my flight."

I nearly passed out when I sat back down. I realized that I had managed to hold my breath as I waited for something magical to occur when I finished pointing my finger.

That was it – after that, with a "thank you" from the judge, I was told to leave the room.

Outside the courtroom, both detectives hugged me. For the first time, I felt like a weight had been lifted from my shoulders, though I was still concerned for my safety and the safety of my family – I had witnessed the seething anger of the Chaney family. The trial made me realize that my involvement had changed many lives, mine included.

"You were magnificent," Detective Petroski said. Detective O'Leary smiled in agreement.

I found out later that both brothers were sentenced to life imprisonment for the murder, and that their appeals were denied.

I returned to Kansas City that very day, relieved that the long trial was over. I knew that no one at my station could ever know of my involvement in the justice system. There were still a few hostesses who tried to catch me off guard about the unanswered mystery of my transfer in 1972.

It made me laugh, each time they tried.

CHAPTER TWENTY-FIVE

THE SENATOR

The flight from Kansas City to St. Louis was consistently full. Only a 248-mile trip by car, the drive on Highway 70 East was fraught with 18-wheelers, testing the will of the most dogged drivers, so when TWA introduced a nonstop, the locals took advantage of the short 30-minute flight. It also served as a backup for the JFK nonstop, which was also consistently overbooked with commuters.

On this day, we were made aware of a local man – a U.S. Senator – who was traveling with his wife and infant. As it was our company policy, parents with children were boarded first. As they began to line up, a TWA gate agent came onto the plane to speak with me.

I often commuted to New York when I was based there, and I knew her as Julia. She said, "I need to ask you for a big favor today – can you make an exception today on the FAA policy about parents using car seats?"

Now I was confident that Julia had to be under the gun to make such a request. Her eyes pleaded with me as she turned slightly and gazed at the lineup of parents waiting their turn to board.

"There's a man standing at the front of the line," she said, "Do you see him?"

As I looked at the line of passengers, a rather distinguished, gray-haired man stood talking to his wife. They were obviously in a deep discussion, probably about their next move.

"Hard to miss him," I replied "So what?"

"Well, he has a baby," she said.

I nodded. "I see that."

"He wants to use a car seat on the plane."

"Not happening," I replied.

"But he's a U.S. Senator from Missouri!" she pleaded.

"So, you want me to put my job on the line for a senator, who not only knows the laws, but who actually helps make them?" *This woman is really losing it*, I thought

I could see the senator straining to hear our conversation, positive, I'm sure, that Julia's relationship with me and his powerful position would win me over. Even the Captain couldn't overrule this decision; in the end the FAA rules were law, and all three of us knew that.

"It's just this one time," she said. "No one will ever know."

"Well, I would know, and you would know, and he would know, and all the other parents standing in line would know." I shook my head, watching his face. I hoped that he would recognize my unspoken determination.

Just as I finished speaking, the senator approached, carrying the car seat. His wife, holding the infant child, stood directly behind him as the child began to wail. Obviously agitated by the sudden screams, the man attempted to walk right past me. I stopped him.

"I'm sorry, sir, but car seats are not allowed to be used on the plane," I said. "You must gate-check it, and the child will sit on your lap for takeoff and landing."

"Well, that's ridiculous!" he sputtered. "Car seats have been mandatory in all cars since 1978. Did you know that?" He was clearly ready for a confrontation. "They save thousands of children's lives in vehicles."

"I agree," I said, "however, the FAA has not approved them for aircraft, so I cannot allow you to use the car seat on this plane."

"Do you know who I am?"

"I've been told you represent Missouri in the Senate."

He spoke over me, saying, "I am a United States senator; my name is Kit Bond. Do you want to see my ID?"

"That won't be necessary, sir; I believe you."

He stared at me as his wife gently attempted to push him along. He didn't budge.

"I cannot believe how incredibly stupid this is," he said, turning to his wife for support. She winced as the baby grabbed her beautifully coiffured hair in its tiny hand.

The passengers seated in First Class were now peeking around each other in an attempt to see what the loud disturbance was. My line wasn't getting any shorter.

"Sir," I said, "I am going to ask you to leave the car seat by the door here and we will make sure its gets to your destination. What is your destination today?" I took a gate tag from my counter as I began to write his name.

"Where? What do you think?"

I forced a smile. "Maybe, Washington D.C.?"

His face was now turning a dangerous shade of red.

"Can we go on the jetway to discuss this so that the other passengers can board?" I asked.

"No, we are going to finish this right here." He stood firmly in front of me, the car seat pressed against my thigh.

I could feel my blood pressure rise. Sadly, I totally agreed with him; the cabin crews had discussed the absurdity of the FAA rules regarding car seats. Our union and that of other airlines had even petitioned for a change in the ruling, but the FAA and the Department Of Transportation had yet to determine the need for a change. Children were to be held in the lap of a parent for takeoff and landing on all US carriers – any moron could determine that this was clearly unsafe in unexpected turbulence or a crash.

And we were the ones who had to enforce this ridiculous rule.

As we stood staring at each other, the senator requested a supervisor.

Passengers, now passing by the senator, smiled and attempted to shake his hand. He kindly reciprocated as he waited for what he hoped would be an overruling.

The supervisor appeared. She knew him, too. "What can I help you with?" she asked.

"This young lady will not allow me to use a perfectly good car seat for my child. Please tell her to let me."

I could tell by the supervisor's face that she was uneasy about her involvement in this decision. "She's following FAA rules, sir. I am sure she feels the same way that you do, but I must back her on this. We will need to check the car seat."

"Ridiculous, simply ludicrous."

"Agreed," I replied.

"Fine."

As I tagged the car seat and he prepared to walk away, he asked for my name and base. I wrote it down, knowing a bad letter would be making its way in my direction. Handing him the note with my name and payroll number, I said, "Sir, if you don't like the rule, do what you do best: go to Washington and change it."

If he did, I have never heard of his involvement in changing the rule. He left the car seat with me and took his First-Class seat. I knew the 30-minute-long flight was going to feel like an eternity with his steely blue eyes watching my every move. Each time I walked past him, I could feel the heat of his anger. I surmised that he was used to winning most of his battles, and I hoped that this encounter would go a long way in the battle for the flight safety of infants.

The bad letter never arrived. His career lasted 14 years where he was a progressive and well-liked senator in Missouri. There is a beautiful bridge named after him. I pass by it regularly, and when I do I recall our conversation.

It took years of suggestions from airline crews to the NTSB, FAA, and DOT before the rules were changed regarding car seats and the protection they provide for our most vulnerable travelers. There were rumors that the airlines were unwilling to agree because parents would balk at the idea of purchasing an additional ticket for an infant. However slowly, and with little fanfare, the FAA eventually allowed specific car seats – ones that had been rigorously tested – to be used on airplanes.

CHAPTER TWENTY-SIX

DIVERSION

Flying in the winter was always tricky; with the promise of unpredictable weather that could play havoc with our flight schedules, bidding on warmer destinations was critical to our peace of mind.

I was fortunate this month to fly on a Boeing 707 into San Francisco from Kansas City. It was a nonstop, and the best part was flying from the icy roads of Kansas City into the warm, ocean laden air of San Francisco. It made working the 'always-full flights' more tolerable.

In addition, the layover was a dream – we stayed at the iconic Mark Hopkins Hotel, which towered over Nob Hill, allowing for magnificent views of the city. The hotel rooms were luxurious, and the location as perfect as you could get for a short layover. It was understandable why this flight could go very senior.

I had traded into this schedule with a very senior friend who had fallen in love with a man in Dayton, Ohio. It must have been true love for her to trade a non-stop overnight flight to San Fran for a six leg DC-9 trip in and out of Dayton during the winter.

During one San Francisco layover, after a deep sleep nestled in luxurious Egyptian linens, I caught one of the famous cable cars down to the wharf with Sally, a woman I was flying with. Once there, we found coffee and freshly made croissants. Languid sea lions warmed their massive bodies on the rocks that lined the bay, occasionally barking to one another and scaring the young children. Sally and I sat and observed the comings and goings of the tourists as they shopped at the various stores at Pier 39, or waited patiently on long lines as a tour boat to Alcatraz slowly returned from the island.

"Have you ever done the tourist thing and visited Alcatraz?" I asked mindlessly.

"Nope," Sally said. "Never been interested enough to get in a boat with a bunch of people on that bumpy ocean filled with sharks."

"I bet they are pretty hungry now that there are no more convicts on the island trying to swim away."

"Right. That's why I plan to stay on land."

After doing some light shopping for fresh vegetables like artichokes and avocados to reward our families with, we headed back to the hotel to dress for our flight.

After stowing our crew kits on the plane, we met the captain in the first-class cabin for our briefing. He shared that the Midwest was enduring massive snowstorms. One city mentioned was St. Louis, and we all felt lucky to avoid the chaos that most certainly was happening there.

As our flight entered Denver airspace, the captain called Agatha, our senior, into the cockpit. He informed her that TWA Operations was diverting our plane to Denver.

This was very unusual; normally this was only done due to an emergency of some sort, but not today – our plane was being commandeered by Operations.

All flights to St. Louis had been canceled for days due to harsh weather and snowstorms. A few hundred people were stranded in Pittsburgh and undoubtedly anxious to return home.

After landing we deplaned our unhappy Kansas City passengers, who had already been accommodated by our agents to fly home on other flights.

We then refueled and departed for Pittsburgh, where we landed at around 7:00 P.M. Our empty plane was met with cabin service and commissary. An exhausted looking gate agent briefed us. "It is utter chaos out there. I cannot begin to tell you how much I appreciate you coming to our aide. Our flight is oversold. That is going to be my problem, not yours."

She handed the passenger manifest to the senior hostess who stared at her quizzically.

The agent continued: "I know, I look a mess. Everyone has been working double shifts. I slept in the crew room last night. This weather started delaying our flights around four days ago, and the worst of it hit yesterday. The passengers are wearing us down – we have already called the police on two people. I am so glad you folks showed up." We handed her a glass of water.

"We heard from crew scheduling that there should be a couple of planes on their way to rescue these people," Agatha said.

"Oh, I hope so. Are you ladies ready to board?"

Agatha nodded. "Send them on."

Just as we started to board, the captain announced that we needed to board quickly since another storm was headed for St. Louis. He was hoping to beat it.

The passengers began to board the plane, and we could tell they were anxious and tired; the normal jovial banter at the door was absent. They looked disheveled as they slowly made their way to their seats. I felt sorry for the two or three mothers holding small babies, and we all made a concerted effort to be as helpful with luggage as much as possible.

The overheads of the Boeing 707 were designed much like a bus – only coats and hats were allowed, and no other luggage was permitted. It seemed like it took longer to board than the thirty minutes the captain had requested, but we were right on the money.

With everyone on board, the gate agent handed us the final paperwork. "There are some angry people out there; I wish I could come with you." She laughed nervously.

As she closed the door, I could hear a big sigh of relief from the cabin.

The captain gave a short announcement, explaining that we had been kidnapped by our company to come and rescue them rather than go home to our families. As they understood, they clapped for us and began to smile.

As I walked through the cabin doing my seatbelt check several passengers reached out to touch my hand. "Thank you, young lady," a man said.

My galley hostess explained that we were serving a full dinner, even though the flight time was under two hours. Agatha came back to inform us that liquor was also free – the captain had authorized it. She cautioned us to keep an eye on the drinkers. "They've all come to know each other," she said. "Sometimes this creates a party atmosphere."

As we taxied to the active runway, I could hear a few passengers beginning to sing. I couldn't quite make out the song, but it was seemed familiar.

They quieted down as we began our takeoff roll, but a moment later there was a flash of fire from the left wing and a loud explosion, and everyone began to scream.

"Compressor stall!" my partner, Jennifer, and I breathed softly.

Immediately the captain slowed the takeoff and turned off the active runway. Jennifer and I stood up and walked through the cabin to calm the passengers. Agatha made an announcement letting the passengers know that the captain would announce what happened in a moment.

Eventually, the captain came on the P.A. "Well, ladies and gentlemen, you have all just experienced a 'compressor stall' better known as an engine backfire. It's rare, but when it happens it sure can make a bad impression. I'm sorry if it scared you. I'm returning to the gate to allow our mechanics to see if we damaged our engine, which is rare in this instance. I'll let you know as soon as I find out."

An audible groan could be heard throughout the cabin. A few passengers began to cry.

After a short check by the mechanics, we were given clearance to depart. The tension in the cabin was palpable. One lady continued to moan as we began our roll for takeoff. Out of nowhere, another woman stood up and began to scream, "I'm scared. Let me off!"

Everyone in the cabin was yelling at her to sit down, but Agatha must have heard the commotion on the plane and called the captain. The plane slowed dramatically, as we began turning off the runway and back to the gate.

The gate agent again opened the door. Six people, including the screaming lady and the moaning lady and their spouses, deplaned. The agent was of course perplexed, but just as the six left, six more passengers boarded replacing them. "Any open seat," the agent told them.

Just as she began to close the door, Agatha got on the P.A. "If you are afraid to go with us, get off now. We are not returning to this gate to let anyone off again."

Again, the passengers clapped in agreement.

As the clapping died down Agatha said, "This is your last chance."

The cabin was silent, so the agent closed the door and off we went for a normal takeoff. No compressor stalls and no screams this time.

We began our liquor service, and each passenger enjoyed two free cocktails. There was a lot of talking going on in the cabin, so dinner service took longer than usual.

Before we realized it the familiar sound of the engines warned us of our immediate descent into St. Louis. We began running up and down the aisle arms fully loaded with used food trays. For the first time in my career, I was forced to throw dirty trays in the lavatory. There was no time to stow them properly – we were too close to landing.

Just as I sat in my jumpseat, I could feel the sound of the big plane touching down. It sounded strange, maybe because of the icy runways. Then I could hear the thrust reversal. It seemed louder than usual and somehow unproductive. Then I realized the plane just wasn't stopping, it was sliding.

After seconds that felt like minutes, we stopped. Massive piles of plowed snow lined the runway, and they became the resting place for our plane. The entire cockpit was nestled in a rather large snowbank; we had used the entire length of the runway in an effort to stop. Fortunately, we were all safe, and it was comical where it not for the need to get to the gate.

The captain met with the mechanics at the front door. A moment later the captain announced to everyone that in order to get to the gate to deplane, we would have to be towed out. That, he said, could take an hour or two. The groan from the cabin was much louder than last time.

The captain then gave the passengers a choice of waiting on a tow or deplaning on air-stairs. They would have to make a short icy walk to the terminal.

It was a majority vote. They all decided to walk. They were somewhat tipsy and so happy to get off the plane and be home safe. It didn't take long to deplane.

The crew were all exhausted, but the captain wanted to meet in the hotel bar for 'coffee' and a debrief. A flight report would need to be written for the company. He wanted to make sure our stories were straight.

When we finally made it to the hotel, the bar and restaurant were full of our passengers. When we walked in there was a roar of laughter and clapping.

It seems their cars were covered with the snow that had made their lives miserable in the first place. It was going to be a long night for them.

We had hotel reservations and while most of the passengers had relatives driving to get them, a few were in the parking lot scraping snow while the rest were continuing the party at the bar.

Everyone was relieved to be home safe. The captain was the star of the show as he shared his stories about compressor stalls.

CHAPTER TWENTY-SEVEN

THE ST. LOUIS TO HAWAII INAUGURATION, 1986

The call came early.

"Good morning, this is crew scheduling. Is this Dianna?" Before I could confirm, he continued: "We have a special assignment for you today." He sounded like he was tittering.

Today? A special assignment? I presumed that perhaps a women's club needed a speaker or such – I had given talks many times at retirement homes.

I was annoyed with the early call, but I tried to remain civil. "Well, what is it?"

"We would like you to work our inaugural nonstop from St. Louis to Honolulu today," he said. "It's a big deal – the press will be there."

"Today?" I whined. "I am just barely legal from my Frankfurt flight." I pulled out my flight log from my overloaded purse, wanting to make sure my block times were correct.

"I understand," he said, "but I just received a sick call, and you are now the only Flight Service Manager legal to fly this flight. I'm really sorry for this last-minute assignment."

Crew schedulers had the unenviable task of juggling unappreciative women's schedules in an effort to keep our planes flying on time; it was a thankless job. Since the strike began, long-standing procedures and protocol were lost in the shuffle. His request was unusual, but not illegal, and I could try and file a grievance with the union, but oh wait! No, I couldn't – the union now hated me.

"Why did I have to be the only Service Manager legal to fly today?" I said to my young daughter who stared up at me with her sweet, quizzical smile. My three-year-old son understood that I was leaving again and had already begun hiding my uniform items throughout the house in a losing battle to keep me home. He was getting more creative each day – the last time he had hidden my hostess wings in a shoe.

"Hawaii," I said to my daughter, "This could be interesting." I had never worked on a flight there, and memos about the new non-stop explained that it was another promotional effort to regain ground in TWA's losing battle for passengers had arrived in our mailboxes earlier that month.

I rushed to repack my suitcase with clean underwear and pantyhose. I fortunately found two clean shirts. The babysitter came quickly, and as I left, I waved goodbye to my screaming baby boy, who always showed his disapproval when I departed.

Reviewing the flight times from Kansas City to St. Louis, I knew I would arrive just in time to check in for the Hawaii flight. It was my habit to always arrive a few hours early to inspect the aircraft for possible commissary issues, but today I would need to trust the commissary supervisors.

The St. Louis Airport was full of eager first-time flyers from the Midwest on their way to the romantic city of Honolulu. Older gentlemen wearing WWII caps juggled suitcases as they followed wives in long dresses with matching bonnets. They all seemed to be dressed for church, and it was a sweet and colorful scene.

The flight had been advertised as "Your Flight of a Lifetime." Most of our passengers would be experiencing not only their first time on an airplane, but also on a 747. A fully-loaded airplane was guaranteed by the ridiculously low fare.

Local journalists looking for a story about the world-renowned 747 mixed into the crowd, and as my crew and I pushed our way to the gate, a few photographers asked us for a photo. We declined – TWA had a strict policy regarding unsolicited photos.

"I'll pay you $100 to let me come on the plane just for two minutes," a young journalist suggested.

"I don't think $100 is worth my job, buddy," I said, and I pushed past him.

On the plane, my crew gathered in first class, awaiting a briefing.

"Good morning," I said, "here we are for another momentous flight on the 747. This is the first non-stop from St. Louis to Honolulu. You all get to be a part of history. "

"Oh hooray," a single sarcastic voice chirped from the group. Laughter followed.

I continued. "We have a full load. We serve sandwiches and more sandwiches in all cabins – you should all have full carts. Please open your liquor carts and make sure you have a full complement of soft drinks and liquor. Check your boarding sheets attached to the carts, and if you have questions or concerns let me know before we start boarding so I can call down for supplies."

I cleared my throat and looked at each crew member. "You are going to encounter many first-time flyers – be patient with them. They will ask questions about the 747 like, 'How long is it?' 'How fast does it fly?' Et cetera, et cetera. I'm handing out a fact sheet about the plane just in case."

"Also, of course liquor is still free, so keep an eye on passengers in your zone. It's a long flight, and some passengers may not be as familiar with the effects of alcohol in flight. I don't want to deal with a bunch of drunk farmers."

Everyone laughed. One hostess from Iowa quipped, "Hey, we know how to hold our liquor!"

We began boarding, and as I stood by the L-1 door, I heard a loud conversation in the queue just outside the plane entrance.

A lady wearing a bonnet was speaking to two men. "I can't believe you would wear something like that in public, and on an airplane even!"

"Well, bitch, we're First-Class passengers; we can wear whatever we want," one man replied.

Another man, probably the woman's husband stood close to her as he yelled, "Don't you use that foul language towards my wife." He was dressed in a suit, but I could see his muscles bulging as he flexed his forearms, moving towards the men.

I left the door and made my way towards the group. As I approached, I saw that the two other men were wearing short and 'wife beater' shirts with coordinating flip flops. One was younger, and the older one sported a white beard and a very hairy chest.

Dividing them from the group, I asked, "May I see your boarding passes?" It was then that I saw raw flesh protruding from where the shorts material should have been.

Daisy dukes, I thought, for *First Class, even*. The backs were also removed from the short shorts, and I was somewhat in shock, having never witnessed this particular fashion statement before.

Well, that's not entirely true – I did observe a couple of men wearing them one night at the entrance of Studio 54 in New York. The infamous disco had become the place to "see and be seen," and people donned outrageous outfits that hopefully would gain them entrance into the club with the equally outrageous discriminating door policy.

"Please follow me," I said, mentally preparing myself for a fight. Not wishing to address their clothing issue in front of the other passengers, I invited them into the First-Class galley. I waived another hostess over to continue checking the boarding passes.

"I have to tell you that I've never seen shorts like yours before," I lied.

The younger man twirled like a marionette, obviously proud of his design. As he did, I could hear the other passengers behind me laughing.

"So, what do you think? Pretty bitchin, eh?" The older man said this admiringly, as he slapped his partner on his bare behind.

Bitchin' – I hadn't heard that word since I left California, and it took me back for a second, but the sound of his slap startled me back into reality.

"I realize you both are comfortable with your look; however, I am not. Even if you were seated in coach – which you aren't – we would still be having this conversation."

"I guess you heard me and the old bitty earlier," the older man said.

"Yes, I did. That conversation is why I cannot allow you on my airplane, especially in First Class, until you change your attire," I said. I was now wondering if the gift shops sold clothing.

"Why? What's the reason? Is it because you don't like our shorts or is it because we're gay?" the older man asked.

"You're gay? I replied, acting surprised. "Your lifestyle has nothing to do with this. We are very tolerant at TWA; we have many gay employees. Your lifestyle is not the problem – your clothing is – it's offensive to the other passengers."

"Well, some of them liked it," the younger man said, "or they wouldn't be staring."

This man was clearly delusional. "Sir," I said. "I don't wish to get into a discussion with you. I'd like to point out that in some cultures, showing your bare buttocks is very offensive and it is so here today in the 'Bible Belt.' And it is my job to address everyone's comfort and safety."

As I waited for their response, I felt a tap on my shoulder. It was a mechanic. "Can I have a word?" he whispered.

"Excuse me," I said to the two men, "I'll be right back."

The mechanic and I walked onto the jetway. "Wow, looks like you have your hands full," he said.

"Yes, I do, but go ahead and give me more bad news." I replied.

"We have a mechanical problem. It shouldn't take too long, but the captain wanted you to know."

"Do I have at least thirty minutes? I asked.

"Oh, it'll be that, at least," he replied. "We have to remove the engine cowling and see if the mice are still asleep." He chortled as he walked away.

"Hilarious," I whispered to myself.

Most of the passengers had already boarded, so I could wait before announcing the delay; there was no point in upsetting everyone. Most of them were busy examining the overhead bins and comfy airplane seats.

I returned to the two men. The reality of the situation had caused the younger man to begin sniffling. He was probably thinking I was going to toss them off the plane.

"I have two options for you," I said. "I can have your luggage sent up for a wardrobe adjustment, or I can remove you from the plane. It's your choice."

"You can do that? Isn't that illegal?" the younger asked.

"We own the plane; we make the rules," I said. I was starting to get annoyed. I had a million other things that needed my attention, including the other 340 passengers.

"Can we wait on the plane while you do that?" the older man asked. "I really don't want to go back into the terminal."

"No, you'll have to go back to the terminal and change your clothes. Our lavatories are locked until after takeoff." I realized I was being petty, but these two were really getting on my last nerve.

"Well, that's just mean," the younger man said, wiping a tear from his cheek.

"It may be mean, but it's my decision," I said. "Talk about it, but don't take too long. My guys need time to dig for your bags. And if we can't get them up here before we go, you'll have to stay here. I'll be right back." I left and quickly made my way upstairs to the cockpit, where I explained my situation to the captain. He didn't need to be part of the decision, but I always let the crew know what was happening downstairs.

"Good job," the captain said. "We saw those yahoos in the terminal and hoped they weren't on our plane. Stand your ground; I have your back."

"Well, here's hoping they make the right decision. I hate writing long flight reports for Carl," I said.

I closed the door to the cockpit and then returned to the jetway, where the two men stood awaiting my arrival. "Well, what's it going to be?" I asked.

The younger man handed me their two bag tags. "Even though we don't agree with you, we really want to go on this flight. We only paid $1,000 roundtrip for First Class, but we don't want to miss this chance" He quipped.

I am sure that I gulped when I heard how little they paid. Our First-Class fares price usually exceeded this miniscule amount.

I had already summoned a baggage handler to wait on the jetway, and he took the tags and was off. Five minutes later, the bags sat next to the men. TWA always loaded First Class bags in a separate cargo bin from regular coach bags which explained the efficiency – the leopard-striped bag tags may have helped to identify them, as well.

I watched as the two men walked back to the terminal to change. A gate agent came down immediately afterwards, asking if I had thrown them off. I think she was hoping I had – she said she wished she had denied them boarding but didn't want to lose her job. "You are fearless!" told me. She didn't know that termination at this moment might have been my preference – I was running out of patience for such nonsense.

Moments later, the two men appeared at the First-Class boarding door. They both had on beautifully-tailored suits and Hawaiian-themed ties; I was impressed. Along with the new suits, they also had attitude adjustments – the younger man apologized, as did the older.

"Your gate agent rechecked our bags. I hope you don't mind," The old man said.

"Not at all. Welcome to TWA!" I replied, ushering them on board.

The liquor flowed as the passengers enjoyed their flight. Passengers seemed to continuously visit each other, so the most difficult part for us was walking down the aisles. They compared their plans for Honolulu with one another, and a large group of WWII vets stood and excitedly reminisced about their experiences before the Japanese attack in 1941.

I had already been informed that we were running low on ice, so I cautioned the hostesses to monitor the ice in their zones. It seemed everyone was drinking, and we even served my first scotch and milk. An older farmer explained that he had never had a drink, but that he wanted to try one. He instantly fell asleep, and his wife was sure he had died.

Two hours before landing, we would normally walk through with soft drinks, but we were out all over the plane. We were also out of ice and plastic glasses.

I felt it was my fault since I had neglected to do a provision check on our supplies. I assumed we had been provisioned for a day flight, but after checking the commissary sheets, there had been a mistake. This flight had been provisioned for a night flight. That explained a lot – passengers drink a lot less on night flights, hence the lack of ice.

We served warm water in paper cups to the many hungover first drinkers, even in first class. It was more than embarrassing. The newsmen in first class feverishly went about composing notes as they sipped their warm water.

As we began our final approach, scores of people stood in the cabin, either still drunk or just stupid. I made a call to the captain to circle until I could get them into their seats.

I made several announcements, and yet they continued to stand, defying me. I guess the lack of additional alcohol had made them defiant.

My threats over the PA did not seem to work. We had sky marshals on board, but this wasn't their job. Finally, after calling the captain, he suggested I scare them a little.

"Ladies and gentlemen," I said, "for those of you on insisting on standing, the captain wants you to know that he will circle until we run out of fuel. Then I guess you can figure the rest out."

They sat then.

My original problems with the two men in First Class dissolved. They hugged me as they walked away, declaring that they enjoyed themselves.

When the jet landed, I made a point of finding the outbound Flight Service Manager. I cautioned her to check her provisioning, because I was sure there had been a mix-up.

Sure enough, her flight would be "over-provisioned" with ice and drinks. After some discussion with the commissary, the issue was resolved. These items were very expensive here on an island, so they needed to stay on the island.

I was thankful for fewer issues on the way back home. Twenty-four hours isn't long enough to absorb the beauty of this island, however.

CHAPTER TWENTY-EIGHT

THE BEGINNING OF THE END

When I began as a TWA hostess, I was young and uninformed, not only about the job that I signed up for at age 20, but about life. In time, I grew in a path paved by strong, independent women. Some felt inclined to lend a hand, others made me learn by tripping over myself, but I respected all of them.

TWA was my family; I loved everything about it. I had passed my sixteenth year at TWA when, one sunny day, I found myself fixing a broken video machine on a 767, and I realized I had reached the pinnacle of my career. I *loved* my job.

I doubt I would have ever left my 'Mother TWA,' were it not for the strike in 1986, led by a woman that I had little, if any, respect for. I had met Vicki, our union leader, years earlier during an arbitration that had failed to defend me. I was assaulted on an airplane, by another flight attendant who had mistaken me for her enemy. The union failed to defend me as the innocent victim. The woman kept her job, and I was left angry and bitter.

Vicki was the mirror image of her nemesis, Carl Icahn, pushy and arrogant. (Of course, these are my feelings, not unlike those that led me to eventually cross the picket line.)

One day, as I stood speaking to a group of my young, impressionable peers in the First-Class cabin of a L1011, I knew instinctively that we were on a path to destruction. As I declared that I would cross the picket line, it was obvious that my unpopular stance was lost on them. I tried to explain that we could not win this one; we were up against a menace. Carl Ichan was a corporate raider with his eyes now set on TWA.

Even though I agreed that higher pay and better work rules were important, I felt that that the timing of the strike was poorly planned. TWA, always cash-strapped, was in no position to give us what we desired at this time. Add the assault by Frank Lorenzo and Carl Ichan in their attempts to overtake TWA, and I imagined that TWA was bailing water and hoping for some common unity to help it survive the onslaughts.

I had participated in TWA strikes earlier in my career, but this one was different. In 1970, when we struck for a short 26 hours, supervisors handed out coffee and donuts as they chatted with the strikers at JFK. The strike that began on November 4, 1973, lasted for 45 days, and although it was a bit more confrontational, the words weren't as caustic and demeaning as the ones from our union, the Independent Federation of Flight Attendants, had been in recent months.

I reminded the group that the pilots, mechanics, and agents, along with our other unions, were not in sympathy with our strike; we were on our own. Explaining that 'new hires' were currently being trained to replace us, I cried out, "Has anyone done their homework on Carl Icahn?"

I had, and I knew he would never give in to our demands. He was a corporate raider, and the number of companies that he had decimated was innumerable. "Pick up a *Wall Street Journal* and read about his conquests," I pleaded.

I declared my stance a second time when the union phone call for strike duty came that night. As I cooked dinner for my children in

Lawrence, Kansas, I cried – I knew my dreams had come to an end, and I knew that I was in for the fight of my life. I would fly and help the company survive as long as I could, even amongst the animosity and rancor.

Days later, with my scheduled duty rest over, TWA called. I think the scheduler was surprised when I cordially responded to his request to make my way to St. Louis. I was instructed that once there I would check in at a hotel near Lambert Field to wait for a flight assignment.

Icahn had approved the merger with Ozark Airlines on March 1, 1986, five days before the strike began. Realizing the chaos that was probably happening at the Kansas City Airport, I decided to purchase a ticket on Ozark Airlines. I was hoping to mitigate my exposure to the TWA strikers, and I also knew that passengers had guarantees that crew members traveling freely did not.

I encountered some resistance as I passed through security. Women I knew were now enemies, and though I had packed my uniform, and I was in street clothes, my crew kit, coat, and briefcase immediately set off the strikers. Several attempted to get a little too close to me. Thankfully, they were rebuffed by the police. Icahn had ordered any striker to be arrested if they attempted to attack us.

I successfully boarded, and as I sat down, I became aware of the stares from one flight attendant. When she passed by me, she whispered, "Fucking scab."

I was startled, never thinking this airline – with only five days in the game – would attack me verbally.

The passengers near me heard it. They stared at me.

When she walked past me a second time, and I said, "Take it back!"

She laughed and said, "You're a fucking scab and you know it."

I was offended that someone who did not know me would make an assumption about me, not to mention how embarrassed I felt.

I had made a point of trying to keep her passengers and her airline out of it, but it was too late.

"I'm on a ticket with rights as a full-fare passenger. You, my friend, are looking for a lawsuit. Take it back," I said.

She walked away, ignoring me as we started our decent into St. Louis.

When I deplaned, I casually knocked on the cockpit door. It opened and I said to the captain. "I need to talk to you when you are available."

I stood outside on the jetway waiting for him. The passengers stared, some smiling, as they slowly deplaned, hoping, I am sure, to see a "cat fight" on the jetway.

Soon the Captain approached and asked what it was that I needed.

"I am a TWA Service Manager," I said. "I am on my way to work, with a full-fare ticket, traveling as your passenger. Obviously, I crossed the picket line today to go to work."

"Obviously." He nodded as I continued.

"One of your flight attendants called me a 'fucking scab' more than once in front of your passengers. I want her to apologize; as a passenger, I am offended and embarrassed by her actions. If she apologizes, I will not contact your management and file a formal complaint with the FAA. That's all I'm asking."

He smiled and nodded his head. "Point her out to me."

I looked down the aisle and saw her leering at me. I pointed to her. "That's her," I said.

He went back into the cabin, and soon she was standing in front of me.

"This lady would like an apology," he said.

"What for?" she pleaded. "I just spoke the truth."

"Apologize." The captain spoke louder now. The deplaning passengers were bumping into each other in an attempt to overhear our conversation.

"I will not. She's a scab."

"Well, I tell you what, if you don't do as I've asked, I will charge you with insubordination."

The three of us stood there together, waiting to see who would back down. Finally, after some trepidation on her part, I received a very half-hearted apology. I thanked the captain and turned to find the hotel.

At the St. Louis hotel, I was met by a TWA scheduler, who heartily shook my hand. "Thank you for being so brave. I know this was a hard decision," he said.

"Why are we working out of here?" I asked.

"Well, the strikers are making life miserable for the hostesses. Management decided to move operations inside this hotel for awhile until things cool down."

"Things will never cool down," I said. "Our union president has an axe to grind. She will lead us all off a cliff." Vicki's hatred of Carl Ichan was matched only by his disrespect of her. He was an old-school male-in-charge, and she was the strong, empowered female leading a group of 5,000 women on a road to victory, she hoped. You could hear the animosity as they spoke to one another.

I went to my assigned room, unpacked my crew kit, and hung up my uniform. I needed to call my family and check in, but before I could, someone knocked on my door.

It was a younger man, Nick, who introduced himself as a scheduler. He proudly told me that he was assigning me a flight to Louisville on a three-day turn.

"That's absurd!" I replied.

"What do you mean?" he asked.

"Did you take the time to look at my qualifications? I am a Service Manager; I am qualified to fly on 747s, L1011s, 767s, 707s, 727s, and DC9s. Why on earth would you use me on a three-day turn and use up my duty hours on a 727? Anyone can fly that. I'm not saying I won't fly this pairing, but I'm asking you to reevaluate your choice."

He stared at me for a split second before saying, "Okay, I'll look and see what I can do."

As I prepared once again to call home, he returned. "How about a San Francisco turn on an L1011? Service Managers are on those, right?" he asked.

"Correct, they are." I smiled. "When does it leave?"

He smiled too. "5:30 P.M."

"Done."

I boarded the hotel van at 3:00 P.M. – I had no idea what lay ahead of me, so I wanted to start early. As I saw the terminal appear, hundreds of women, most of them in uniform, walked slowly, carrying signs, and shouting in unison.

Somehow the driver managed to circumvent the strikers by driving to the back of the terminal. Several police officers met our van – our new CEO was serious about protecting his workers. The officers checked our newly issued IDs, checking for the new security stamps emblazoned on them.

The terminal was quieter than usual, and some passengers had changed their travel plans but not on my flight – it was full.

As I boarded my aircraft, I thought, *The quiet before the storm*. I checked the preloaded meals and liquor carts – there were rumors that some sympathetic commissary employees were sabotaging the liquor carts by loading them incorrectly, in an effort to make life even more miserable for us.

The L1011 was a fantastic nightmare of an airplane; I wasn't fond of her from a Service Manager point of view. All carts were stored in the galley, which was in the belly under first class. It was serviced by two sets of elevators, which we called lifts – Not to be confused with elevators located on the tail of the airplane.

Today, without an experienced galley hostess, I knew that I would be working my position in addition to the galley, as someone was needed to send the carts up. *This is my punishment for crossing the line*, I thought.

I discovered that the cabin crew – fellow 'scabs' – were all "18-day wonders," newly hired and trained for a minimum of 18 days to meet FAA qualifications. I was not blessed with one experienced hostess.

They were all cheerful and giddy as I attempted to perform my first briefing with an entire crew of newbies.

"Listen up, ladies," I said. "I know this is all fun and games for you, but you need to listen." I had to quieten them down a few more times as they giggled their way through the briefing.

Fortunately for us, and unfortunately for the First-Class passengers, the food service would be limited to sandwiches and salads. Coach cocktails would be free. It made my job easier, not having to count the liquor money, but I knew some passengers would take advantage of the younger, less experienced hostesses and drink over their limits. I made a point of not announcing the 'free liquor' policy to the passengers as I was hoping to slow down any perspective boozers.

"Keep an eye on your drinkers," I said. "If someone seems drunk and insists on another drink, contact me. I'll handle it."

The flight seemed to be going well, until an early landing fouled my timing. I still had around three carts missing from the downstairs galley, and I could hear the carts, untethered from their giant floor magnets. I imagined them moving freely down the aisle as the plane slowly descended into San Francisco.

When I attempted to use the lifts to go upstairs, I found the doors had been left ajar – the elevators were designed to stop if the doors were not closed completely. As I called on the inter-phones, attempts at getting a response from anyone upstairs proved fruitless. My overhead announcements were also unproductive.

I called the captain and asked if he could circle until I could get the situation under control, and I could hear the anger in his response – pilots don't like to get out of line for landing, especially in San Francisco.

Just as I had decided to use the emergency exit located under the rug in First Class, the galley door opened, and a lone cart appeared. I quickly stowed it and rode upstairs to evaluate the cabin. My 'crew' was flirting with the passengers, and I am sure the look on my face was a clear indication of how my day was going. After much scrambling, I was able to tell the captain we were ready for landing.

A crew bus, splattered with eggs, secretively delivered us to an unscheduled hotel. TWA had changed our hotel at the last moment to confuse the strikers in San Francisco. The layover would be for a short eight hours.

"I want you all down in the lobby at 4:00 A.M. for a briefing," I said as we prepared to leave the bus.

"What?" an unnamed hostess shouted from the back of the bus.

"Isn't our flight leaving at seven? Why four?"

"Because you all need a briefing. See you in the lobby at four." I left to sign them in at the check in counter.

I knew they were angry, but it had been a trying day, and I was exhausted. Another day like today couldn't be tolerated. I wondered what they had been taught in that 18-day class.

At 4:00 A.M., the lobby was full of sleepy new hires with one flight under their belts. I had made a list of things that needed addressing on their first flight, and we discussed the lack of attention and overly enthusiastic flirting that I had seen.

"Get you job done, check your cabin for trash and seat belts, and then and only then can you flirt, *if* you have time."

Fortunately, it was a good discussion. We all went to breakfast, and I hoped we had bonded in a small way.

After succumbing to a few thrown eggs, we made it to our gate intact. As we entered the jetway, a few supervisors stood at attention, lining the walls, clipboards in hand, prepared to follow the women onboard to brief them.

I held my hand up and said, "Wait. These ladies have been up since 4:00 A.M. getting briefed. Stand back and watch them."

The moment was a testament to the loyalty we all had for an airline that truly deserved it.

CHAPTER TWENTY-NINE

THE TAKEOVER

"TWA was the Marilyn Monroe of the airlines:
an American icon done in by powerful men who wanted a
piece of its magic. Glamorous, tragic, gone before its time."
—Elaine X. Grant, "TWA: Death of a Legend," *St. Louis Magazine*

As soon as Carl Icahn took over the day-to-day operations of TWA, small cracks of mismanagement began to form in the day-to-day operation of our company. It was obvious that those in the halls of 605 Third Avenue, our corporate headquarters in New York, were no longer in charge.

When Carl added his minions to the organization, they were charged with cutting TWA's overhead in any legal way possible. The personal threats from the striking flight attendants intensified, and he warned that the police were to arrest anyone interfering with the scabs.

As passenger loads dropped dramatically due to the strike, we knew the future of TWA was tenuous. Passengers would not risk buying airline tickets when there were no guarantees that the airline would actually be flying.

We also noticed that the customers' amenities suffered as well – the three delicious choices of food for coach passengers were now reduced to one, and customer comforts such as pillows and blankets seemed to be slowly disappearing. It was an adjustment for everyone.

The change that affected us the most, however, was the reassignment of layover hotels. They were not the four- and five-star hotels that we were accustomed to, rather, they were more along the lines of a Days Inn. Gone was the concierge that catered to our every need, as well as the late-night room service – I missed that the most. There's nothing like a well-made club sandwich at midnight following a twelve-hour duty day.

I continued to fly and to try to train my younger peers as I worked my way into deciding to leave a job I so dearly loved.

On January 28, 1986, I was unfortunate enough to witness the Challenger Space Shuttle break apart, 73 seconds into its flight, as I sat on a Delta jet descending into Miami. It was a harbinger of things to come. Tragically, on April 2, 1986, a bomb exploded on a TWA jet while at 15,000 feet over the Ionian Sea. A woman affiliated with the Arab Revolutionary Cells in sympathy to Muammar Gaddafi had hidden a bomb under a passenger seat on an earlier flight. Though the quick-thinking TWA pilot was able to land the 727 safely, the explosion killed four people and injured seven.

Three days later, a bomb exploded in a bar in West Berlin, killing three people, including two American servicemen, and injuring 230 other innocent people. Muammar Gaddafi claimed responsibility.

On April 15, President Ronald Reagan ordered 'Operation El Dorado,' a strike force that bombed Gaddafi's home. The revolutionary escaped, remaining on the run until 2011 when he was finally captured and killed by rebel forces.

While all this was going on, the State Department was warning crews to expect possible protests in retribution for the bombing. Days later in London, my 767 crew and I were awakened from our sleep as a large anti-American protest encircled our hotel shouting "American Baby Killers." Supposedly the airstrike on Muammar's home had killed a baby, though it was later reported that the story was a ruse to get sympathy.

Operations in Paris ordered all crews to return to the airport. It seems threats against Americans had increased overnight. Half asleep, we boarded buses in route to the airport, sleeping on our plane until it was time to leave for JFK. My crew, being very young, thought this was exciting and even fun. They should have realized how dangerous our situation was.

Then to make matters worse, on April 26, the small city of Pripyat was rocked with an explosion. This explosion – soon to be world news – was in a nuclear power plant named Chernobyl. The winds that blew over Europe were feared to contain contamination from the nuclear site.

In May of 1986, I began my walk down a jetway in St. Louis to board a flight to Frankfurt, followed by another very young crew. As I got closer to the plane, there were tell-tell signs that the plane had not been cleaned. I could see the large trash bins pulled from storage and blocking the door, and I instinctively knew that something was amiss.

I instructed my crew to return to the terminal to wait for me; I didn't wish to involve them in any discussions I might have with these cleaners, who I knew were very sympathetic to the unions' cause. Small imperceptible protests like this by certain groups had an impact on our ability to get our planes out on time.

As I entered the front door of my airplane, I saw all the cleaners sitting back and drinking and eating leftovers from the flight before, their feet firmly propped up on the backs of the first-class seats. They were watching baseball on our newly installed video machines, which could pick up local stations in the US.

"Hey guys, we're boarding in fifteen minutes," I said. There were at least ten men in the group – some were from other flights, probably on their lunch breaks and taking advantage of the opportunity to see the ball game. This wasn't unusual, but this plane was leaving in an hour.

I received no reply.

This had been happening to other Service Managers, and to help us combat this behavior, the pilots had revealed a small video shutoff switch hidden in the cockpit. I was reticent about using it, since I knew it would cause a standoff, but this was part of crossing a picket line that I had anticipated.

So, I flipped the switch, then walked out on the jetway and called operations on the jetway phone. I asked to speak with my captain, who soon answered.

"Just a minute, sir," I said.

As I stood there, a very large employee exited the airplane, walking towards me in a "raging bull" style; he was angry. I knew him and he knew me, and we had always had a good relationship, but no woman in her right mind turns off a man's baseball program.

"Why'd you do that?' he shouted, loud enough for everyone in Operations to hear.

"You need to clean my plane. It's time to board the passengers, and we have a full load. We need all of the forty-five minutes," I replied.

"Well, you should have thought of that before you turned off our ballgame" He turned back towards the plane.

"Are you going to clean now?" I asked.

"It's going to take us a good thirty minutes. This plane is really a stinker." He laughed.

"That's not funny. Look, I've got enough on my plate with the strike and Gaddafi protestors in London. I can't even eat the lettuce because of Chernobyl poisoning the water."

I thought he might laugh at my dark humor, as he had done in the past, but he did not. "Not my problem," he said, walking closer to me. "But if you ever mess with our TV again, I'm going to personally remake your face."

"Are you threatening me?" I said loud enough for all over the phone to hear. The men from the plane were now lining up on the jetway.

"Not threatening, promising." As he said this, his big baseball mitt of a hand shot so close to my face that I could feel the blood rushing into it.

Then he turned to return to the plane. It was then that the local police piled onto the jetway, along with the captain.

"We heard it all," the captain said.

The cleaners ultimately did their job, though our plane was late departing. I never learned if the man that threatened me was punished, but I doubt it. His union was much stronger than mine.

CHAPTER THIRTY

GOODBYE YELLOW BRICK ROAD, 2001

The summer sun was playing havoc on my eyes, and I squinted at the sound of a plane flying overhead. I longed for a glimpse of my beloved airline.

Having just dropped off my youngest daughter at her Montessori school, I dreaded returning to the quiet house that awaited me. I had released my longtime babysitter; I was no longer working so managing the lives of three little children was less complicated than it once had been. There were horse riding lessons and piano lessons to organize, of course. And the myriad birthday parties loading up my underused social calendar – flying had always been my excuse for not attending parties.

At home I opened my old recipe folder, which was stuffed with pieces of interest torn from old international magazines. A chocolate chip recipe from Audrey Hepburn caught my eye – perhaps it was more delicious than the trusty Hershey's recipe on the package of chocolate chips. A cassolette recipe was on the other side. Did I pick the recipe for the cassolette or the cookie? Most likely for the cookie.

I wondered if I was missing my children the day I tore that page out. The recipe was dated 1976, and apparently it had once occupied a small corner of a French magazine named *Voici*. I realized that I would now have more time to rummage through the unread articles and recipes that had been sitting for years waiting to be rediscovered.

I genuinely hoped TWA would achieve the rosy business forecasts that Carl Icahn had promised. Instead, I watched each month as another bloom fell from the once vibrant company.

My nights were occupied with dreams of films of my former job. They were so real that I often was awakened by my own quiet sobs. The scale tipped in the favor of my decision to leave, as the job had become acrimonious, and besides, my children needed me home. They had spent enough of their young years waving goodbye to me.

I invited a small group of airline friends to my home for lunch – I was curious about the real situation regarding TWA after my departure. Elinor, Amy, Sally and Jennifer sat at my dining room table; of the four women, two were still angry at me for crossing the picket line. I never expected any of them to respond to my invitation, but curiosity regarding my demise must have gotten the better of them.

A vase with recently picked roses filled the small dining room with hope.

"Well, girls what's happening?" I asked as I poured wine from a fancy decanter I had purchased in Rome years earlier.

"Carl has really turned the tables on us," Amy said. "Sometimes, I wonder if we might have made a mistake by opening the door for him. Perhaps Lorenzo might have been a better choice."

Frank Lorenzo was a famous union buster from Continental Airlines who also made a bid for TWA at the same time as Carl Icahn but lost. The TWA unions were understandably opposed to his style of management and had voted him out.

"You are kidding yourself if you think we could have stopped him by voting for Lorenzo," I said. "He's a corporate raider; that's what he does. He had his eye on us long ago. He studied us and leaped on us like a hungry wolf." I was probably a lot more descriptive than I had meant to be.

"Did you read the latest article about TWA?"

"No."

"The news has just been announced that he has taken us private. He pocketed a cool $469 million, leaving TWA in debt for $540 million. "We are now swimming in a pool of debt and barely keeping our head above the water," she said as she gulped down her wine". "It was his hidden goal all along to liquidate our assets for his greater good." She continued.

Elinor, who sat next to me, added, "Plus, he's announced at a board meeting that he plans to remake TWA into a budget airline."

"Read this." Sally handed me a newspaper that she had procured in New York city on a layover. She read the copy from an ad: "The World is a Bargain if You Know Where to Shop."

"He's getting ready to do something big. We just don't know what," she said.

My heart ached when I read the ad for myself. TWA must have felt like a jilted lover.

"Did you know he promised the pilots union that he's buying 100 new planes? He purchased 12." Sally spat as she spoke.

"I hate him," Amy said. "He treats us like a cash cow. We can't serve the passengers properly anymore. He's cut our provisioning, and everyone is an angry mess. You were so smart to quit."

"I'm sorry," I said. "This isn't fair. As much as I don't like Carl, I'm even more angry at our management for allowing us to become so weak that we could be taken over so easily."

After a pregnant silence, I asked, "Can we talk about something else?"

Later, after the others left, Amy confided that she had decided to retire. "I'm not waiting for the bastard to destroy all of my dreams."

We hugged, and as I saw them depart, I knew we would most likely never see each other again.

The first death blow came with the sale of the London routes to American Airlines for $449 million. The London routes were the lifeblood of TWA, and now American would feast on them.

TWA limped along, fighting each new financial battle like the brave soldier it was until, like Pan Am Airlines, it would fall from the sky. On July 17, 1996, a TWA 747 exploded eight miles off the coast of Long Island. For years the cause was officially attributed to a faulty fuel tank, but employees, when asked, were confident that a missile strike from somewhere in the ocean had destroyed our plane, along with 230 human beings.

Then, one year after 9/11, TWA flew her last flight from Kansas City to St. Louis. My hope for TWA and its thousands of loyal employees vanished with that flight.

But I will always have my memories. I am forever reminded of my training daily. Still unable to cook with my hair down, I warm coffee cups before serving, and I always fold a napkin just so to nestle my warmed bread. I can no longer allow anyone to stand behind me in my galley, er kitchen. I sometimes forget that TWA also taught me how to rescue passengers from a burning plane, save a small child from choking, or negotiate with a hijacker.

After my retirement, my days soon melded into the day-to-day necessity of running a household with a husband and three children. My profession was no longer a topic of conversation with new friends and neighbors; I was now a wife and a mom.

I blame no one for TWA's demise – not Howard Hughes for promising us the moon with his millions or Carl Icahn for his small betrayals. Many other airlines fell by the wayside after deregulation. It was just our time.

It was a great ride. The love I have for this airline and all it gave me will never be surpassed. It was my mother, my father, and my best friend. I reciprocated by always arriving early for my flights, striving to improve my skills, and showing respect for the passengers who paid mightily for each opportunity to ride on a TWA jet.